THE
MEXICAN
COOKBOOK

THE
MEXICAN
COOKBOOK

Sue Style

Hamlyn

London · New York · Sydney · Toronto

For the many friends
who helped me with this book
and most of all
for that best of friends
the Badger

Other titles in this series:

Complete Indian Cookbook by Michael Pandya
Florence Greenberg's Jewish Cookbook
Regional Chinese Cookbook by Kenneth Lo

ACKNOWLEDGEMENTS

The publishers would like to thank the following
for the loan of accessories and equipment for
photography:

David Mellor, 4 Sloane Square, London SW1
The Craftsmen Potters Assoc. of Gt. Britain,
William Blake House, Marshall Street, London W1
Elizabeth David, 46 Bourne Street, London SW1

Photography by Martin Brigdale
Line illustrations by Joyce Tuhill

First published in 1984 by
The Hamlyn Publishing Group Limited
London · New York · Sydney · Toronto
Astronaut House, Feltham, Middlesex, England

© Copyright Sue Style 1984

ISBN 0 600 32410 9

Phototypeset in Monophoto Century Schoolbook by
Tameside Filmsetting Limited, Lancashire, England

Printed in Italy

Illustrated on front cover *chiles en nogada* (page 100)
Illustrated on back cover *cebiche* (page 39)

CONTENTS

Useful Facts and Figures

Notes on metrication

In this book quantities are given in metric and Imperial measures. Exact conversion from Imperial to metric measures does not usually give very convenient working quantities and so the metric measures have been rounded off into units of 25 grams. The table below shows the recommended equivalents.

Ounces	Approx g to nearest whole figure	Recommended conversion to nearest unit of 25
1	28	25
2	57	50
3	85	75
4	113	100
5	142	150
6	170	175
7	198	200
8	227	225
9	255	250
10	283	275
11	312	300
12	340	350
13	368	375
14	396	400
15	425	425
16 (1 lb)	454	450
17	482	475
18	510	500
19	539	550
20 ($1\frac{1}{4}$ lb)	567	575

NOTE: When converting quantities over 20 oz first add the appropriate figures in the centre column, then adjust to the nearest unit of 25. As a general guide, 1 kg (1000 g) equals 2.2 lb or about 2 lb 3 oz. This method of conversion gives good results in nearly all cases, although in certain pastry and cake recipes a more accurate conversion is necessary to produce a balanced recipe.

Liquid measures The millilitre has been used in this book and the following table gives a few examples.

Imperial	Approx ml to nearest whole figure	Recommended ml
$\frac{1}{4}$ pint	142	150 ml
$\frac{1}{2}$ pint	283	300 ml
$\frac{3}{4}$ pint	425	450 ml
1 pint	567	600 ml
$1\frac{1}{2}$ pints	851	900 ml
$1\frac{3}{4}$ pints	992	1000 ml (1 litre)

Spoon measures All spoon measures given in this book are level unless otherwise stated.
Can sizes At present, cans are marked with the exact (usually to the nearest whole number) metric equivalent of the Imperial weight of the contents, so we have followed this practice when giving can sizes.

Oven temperatures

The table below gives recommended equivalents.

	°C	°F	Gas Mark
Very cool	110	225	$\frac{1}{4}$
	120	250	$\frac{1}{2}$
Cool	140	275	1
	150	300	2
Moderate	160	325	3
	180	350	4
Moderately hot	190	375	5
	200	400	6
Hot	220	425	7
	230	450	8
Very hot	240	475	9

NOTE: WHEN MAKING ANY OF THE RECIPES IN THIS BOOK. FOLLOW ONLY ONE SET OF MEASURES BECAUSE THEY ARE NOT INTERCHANGEABLE.

Key to Ingredients on Pages 10–11

1 onions
2 squash
3 pinapples
4 watermelon
5 garlic
6 *chorizo*
7 assorted fresh chillies
8 fresh green chillies
9 dried corn husks
10 banana leaves
11 pomegranates
12 cloves
13 sultanas [raisins]
14 star anise
15 saffron strands
16 black peppercorns
17 dried *chiles anchos*
18 dried *chiles pasillas*
19 assorted dried red chillies
20 dried *chiles guajillos*
21 root ginger
22 plain flour
23 peanuts

24 red kidney beans
25 black beans
26 hazelnuts
27 *tortilla* (corn) flour
28 pecan nuts
29 walnuts
30 pinto beans
31 vanilla beans
32 cinnamon sticks
33 courgettes [zucchini]
34 French [green] beans
35 avocados
36 limes
37 green peppers
38 fresh coriander
39 parsley
40 bay leaves
41 fresh thyme
42 tomato
43 papayas
44 bananas
45 mangoes
46 tangerines

INTRODUCTION

'Mexican cuisine is, at its finest, one of the most interesting in the world . . .'* The trick is to find the finest – not as easy as you might think. Anyone who's ever been lucky enough to travel to Mexico will know that it's not to be found in the type of restaurant that tourists would frequent, and it's little consolation to be told that *real* Mexican food can only be had in people's homes, or in the local market: you may never get an invitation to the former, and the prospect of Moctezuma's Revenge following a visit to the latter might deter you, tempting though it all looks and smells.

In the States, people have known and enthused about something called 'Mexican food' for many years. However, it's as well to keep in mind that *tacos* as served in the average fast-food chain bear about as much resemblance to the real thing as *minestrone* in Manchester – and are about as representative – and that *chili con carne* came from Texas, not Mexico. . .

Elsewhere, Mexican cooking has still to be seriously discovered, and as our culinary horizons are constantly extended, and as most of us can now find limes, mangoes, fresh chillies and corn in the local supermarket, the possibility of experimenting with new, original and exciting dishes from other cultures is greater than ever.

My sources and inspirations for this book were many: Socorro, the hairdresser, who as the hairdryer reached a mounting crescendo would patiently explain the finer points of chilli peeling and sauce preparation; maids such as Audelia, Emilia and Esther, each from a different area of Mexico and each bringing with her the particular flavour of her own *tierra*; cooks and chefs from behind the scenes in homes and restaurants who were delightedly surprised to find a foreigner so interested in their food; a series of much-loved, dog-eared, crumbling paperback manuals collected on happy Saturday morning browsings in provincial markets; my own practical teaching experiences with faithful guinea pigs both in Mexico and back in Europe; and perhaps most importantly, Diana Kennedy, a fellow Englishwoman whose book *The Cuisines of Mexico*† awakened my interest in the first place.

In two important respects the recipes differ from the originals as given to me: firstly, I have assumed that you don't have an Audelia or an Emilia patiently chopping away in the background, and have therefore simplified preparation and cooking methods accordingly, making fullest use of all the modern kitchen aids available (especially the food processor). Secondly, I have drastically reduced the quantity of oil and fat specified originally, as well as that of sugar in the dessert section. They are excessive to our tastes, unnecessary to the success of the finished dish and, of course, out of step with modern ideas about good food for good health. In all other ways I have kept each dish as close to its origins as possible, and in the very few cases where an original ingredient is really unavailable, I have suggested alternatives which have preserved the flavour and texture of the dish as it was conceived.

Mexican food is like its people: warm, colourful, a blend of many cultures and influences, noisy, explosive, often surprising, always a little imprecise. This book sets out to distil a little of all these flavours into a selection of dishes for different occasions which can be prepared with ease and authenticity in a non-Mexican kitchen.

*Quentin Crewe's *International Pocket Food Book*, published by Mitchell Beazley, 1980.

†*The Cuisines of Mexico*, by Diana Kennedy, published by Harper & Row 1972.

Special Cooking Methods

As a genre of cookery, Mexican food is wholesome and satisfying not just because of what goes into it, but also because of how you arrive at the finished dish. Many of the ingredients are high-protein, high-fibre foods, but also the fast frying of the concentrated purées which form the basis of sauces gives an incredible intensity of flavour, and a consistency due solely to natural reduction of liquids by fast boiling, or the addition of nuts or seeds as thickening agents: flour is never used.

Equipment

For all the chopping, blending and pounding that needs to be done, it makes sense to invest in a **food processor** if you don't already have one. It helps with a lot of otherwise very tedious chopping chores, since Mexican food is (in Mexican homes anyway) rather labour-intensive.

I'm assuming you already have a **blender** which will be in constant use for sauces (which start out life as purées of tomato/chilli/spices/onion/garlic); in addition I would recommend a **pestle and mortar**, preferably the Mexican *molcajete*, a sort of Aztec blender on three legs, not the kind whose surface is as smooth as the proverbial baby's bottom, where everything you try to grind slithers and bounces about or oozes up the sides. Mexican pestles and mortars are made of sterner stuff – rough volcanic stone – in which in a matter of seconds you can reduce peppercorns to a heap of trembling dust, or chillies and garlic to a pulp.

No frighteningly precise measurements are needed in Mexican cooking, in fact more often than not, *no hay reglas fijas*, which loosely translated means that there are no hard and fast rules. The piece of equipment I use most is a **Pyrex measuring jug**, which gives metric, Imperial and cup measurements.

As sauces are arrived at by first toasting or grilling [broiling] the main protagonists (chillies, tomatoes, seeds, nuts, spices, onion, garlic), you will need **griddles** or **heavy frying pans**, and a **grill [broiler]** or **gas burner** in order to arrive at charred green chillies and peppers. Some **metal tongs** are also useful, in order to minimize the danger of charred fingers. After blending the toasted or grilled [broiled] ingredients, they are often strained, so a **wire sieve** or **food mill** is useful.

For frying sauces, a step you will meet time and time again, a **sauteuse** or **deep, heavy frying pan** or **shallow flameproof casserole** is essential, plus a **splatter shield**: the secret of the flavour is to have the fat nearly smoking when the puréed sauce goes in, so there's a dramatic hiss and splatter, and resultant mess.

Page 9 clockwise, from top left: soufflé dishes, charlotte mould, ring mould, colander, frying pan, metal tongs, food mill, tortilla press, *molcajete*, gratin dish and metal sieve
Previous page raw ingredients used in Mexican cooking (see also page 7)
Left preparation for *tortillas de maíz* (page 17)

Keep your **knives** razor sharp – it speeds everything up and it's a pity to waste time hacking away at things with a blunt blade when a sharp one would do the job in half the time. Lots of **paper towels** also come in handy to mop up any excess fat.

A **steamer**, or **large, deep spaghetti pan** into which you can fit some sort of **rack** or **frying basket** with room for boiling water underneath will be needed for *tamales* (steamed cornmeal parcels), or you could use a large **double boiler**. A **pressure cooker** could also be used to speed up the beans a bit, and for reducing the cooking times specified for the *flans* (caramel creams) to a third.

Plenty of **big, long gratin dishes** (earthenware or enamelled cast iron) will come in handy for all the stuffed *tortilla* dishes. To make *tortillas*, you can get by with a **rolling pin** and **plastic bags**, but for cornmeal *tortillas* the best you can do is to employ a **metal** or **wooden tortilla press**.

For sausage-making (in case you can't easily buy *chorizos* which are called for in a number of recipes) the **sausage-making attachment** to your mixer saves a lot of hassle. I remember hysterical sessions with various maids as we struggled to force pounds of rather reluctant minced [ground] pork and spices through slightly questionable-looking devices into sausage casings.

For the desserts section, **charlotte moulds** or **soufflé dishes** are in constant use for the *flans* (caramel creams), while **ring moulds** double up for desserts and are also used for making rice, beans and vegetable purées look a bit more dressy.

Otherwise all you need is great enthusiasm, energy, and above all a love of fine food.

The Mexican Meal

Mexicans love eating, make no mistake about that. Their main meal, lunch, is scheduled some time between 2 and 5 p.m. (scheduled to begin, that is). It's a rather major affair consisting firstly of soup, then an entrée (or 'dry soup' as it is called, i.e. a rice or pasta dish, or tortilla casserole), or maybe an egg or fish dish (sometimes both). After this comes the main course, called (advisedly) the *plato fuerte* or 'strong dish'. There follows a separate vegetable dish, and of course, the ubiquitous beans; sometimes a little snack creeps in here just to keep the wolf from the door. Finally there is a gentle dessert to soothe the stomach and calm the digestion.

Beside this marathon, the other meals – early breakfast (spartan), mid-morning brunch (a decent repast) and supper (negligible) – pale into insignificance. Of course there are also the *antojitos* or 'little hankerings' which can conveniently be snatched on any street corner or in any market at any time of the day or night when the spectre of hunger menaces . . . I'm not suggesting that you embark on such a programme, unless maybe at a weekend after serious training at high altitudes and severe fasting, and have tailored meal suggestions accordingly.

All recipes have been calculated to serve 4–6 people, in the context of a non-Mexican's interpretation of the three-course meal, unless otherwise indicated.

GLOSSARY

So as not to frighten you off at the outset, you might need any of the following:

Avocados – either the dark, hard-skinned ones or the brighter green, smooth-skinned ones. Often sold rock-hard, so plan in advance: wrap in newspaper and leave in a warm, dark place till ripe.

Bananas and **banana leaves,** if you're lucky enough to find them.

Beans – pinto, red or black, preferably dried but canned will do.

Cheese – Parmesan, a sharp and a mild Cheddar, and a crumbly, white fresh cheese are all used extensively.

Chillies – fresh green and red, any size you can find. Remember that the heat is in the seeds, so if in doubt, or if you only want a warm glow rather than a fire-eating effect, remove the seeds. The dried chillies called for in the book are *ANCHO, GUAJILLO, MULATO, PASILLA* and *CHIPOTLE*. Don't be fooled into thinking that chillies are merely hot – each has a very distinct and delicious flavour. If you really can't find them, substitute 1 tablespoon chilli powder for each chilli in the recipe. It's not at all the same, but if it's the only way you can do it, then beggars can't be choosers. Canned pickled *jalapeño* peeled chillies and peeled green chillies are fairly easily available, the former being fiery hot and the latter rather mild. Look out also for *chiles chipotles en escabeche* or *adobados*.

Chocolate – any dark, semi-sweet brand.

Chorizo – spicy sausage which can be found in Spanish and Italian specialty shops, or make your own from the recipe in the pork section.

Chow chow or **chayote** – a variety of squash, mild-tasting. Substitute kohlrabi if you can't find it.

Cooking fats – lard is most often used in Mexican dishes, also groundnut, safflower and sunflower oil. Butter is very seldom used.

Coriander – one of the most commonly-used herbs in Mexican food.

Courgettes [zucchini] – another variety of squash, and indigenous to Mexico. In Mexico they come in round as well as long varieties, for which the seeds can now be obtained here, too. If you grow your own or have a friendly market gardener nearby, you can also harvest your own **courgette [zucchini] flowers** which figure in a number of recipes. Use only the male flowers (which grow on rather spindly stalks) rather than the female ones (which grow on nice fat little courgettes [zucchini] in the making) and don't pick them all: such bad luck on the bees, and anyway you won't get any babies if you pick all the fathers.

Cream – double [heavy], single [light] and sour. Commercially sour cream tends to go grainy when baked, so make your own *crème fraiche* by adding 2 tablespoons buttermilk, sour cream or plain yogurt to 250 ml/8 fl oz whipping cream, warming to less than blood heat, then leaving, covered, in a warm place to thicken.

Epazote – *Chenopodium ambrosioides*, a very distinctive-tasting herb, native to Mexico and for which there is no substitute. Get the seeds or a cutting from someone who grows it; it flourishes here, too.

Garlic – extensively used. Much of the garlic used in Europe is actually imported from Mexico.

Green tomatoes or *tomates verdes*, of the Physalis family, i.e. not simply an unripe green tomato. They are nicely sharp and acidy, and green gooseberries are a very plausible substitute. Often used with pork or oily fish to provide a foil for the richness of the meat or fish. They also grow well here if you can get the seeds.

Herbs – bay, marjoram, oregano, thyme, parsley (especially the flat-leaved variety).

Huitlacoche – *Ustilago maydis* or corn smut, a silvery-grey fungus which grows on corn cobs, immensely prized in Mexican cooking. Can be bought in cans, but occurs naturally worldwide wherever maize [corn] grows.

Limes – a universal seasoning, even used on the breakfast boiled egg.

Mangoes – the most marvellous and exotic of tropical fruits, often sold rock-hard here (cf. avocados), so ripen in the same way.

Nuts – almonds, walnuts, pecans, peanuts (preferably raw unsalted), pine nuts and hazelnuts are all extensively used, both as thickening agents for sauces, and in desserts.

Olives – green only, used in sauces and as garnish.

Onions – ordinary and spring onions [scallions].

Oranges – both Seville and ordinary varieties.

Papayas – always with the regulation squeeze of lime, and they make a wonderful sorbet.

Peppers – green or white, very occasionally red, and always grilled [broiled] and peeled before use, (see page 54).

Pineapples – much used both in meat dishes and in desserts.

Plantains – very large, menacing-looking bananas, usually green, which have to be cooked to be edible. Try West Indian specialty shops or markets. Prepared as a garnish or cooked with meat or occasionally fish.

Pomegranates – the seeds are much-used as a garnish and in salads to give a bit of crunch. Redcurrants could be substituted at a pinch.

Quince – one of the many Spanish exports to the New World, used to make quince cheese.

Rice – any long-grain variety, but not pre-prepared.

Seeds – especially sesame and pumpkin, as thickening agents, and sprinkled on top as garnish.

Spices – aniseed, cinnamon (best as lengths of bark), whole cloves, cumin seeds, black peppercorns, paprika, vanilla pods [beans], saffron.

(Sweet)corn – the absolute, fundamental, basic ingredient which goes into just about everything, in one form or another, whether as tortillas, or the dough for *tamales*, or as corn kernels.

Sultanas [raisins] – used in savoury and sweet dishes.

Tomatoes – central to Mexican cooking. Use large meaty ones, not tiny salad ones, or in emergencies or in the depths of winter you can resort to canned tomatoes.

Tortillas – two sorts, corn and wheat. Make your own*, using the special maize or corn flour for tortillas which can be found in specialty shops (*harina para tortillas*, or Quaker Masa Harina), and ordinary white flour for the wheat ones. The canned corn tortillas are absolutely not to be recommended.

Vinegar – white wine or cider.

Yogurt – although not typically Mexican, I have quite often suggested substituting yogurt for sour cream as a garnish for dishes – it's easier on the body and the purse, and has the same effect: to provide a sharp, cool contrast to a rich, hot sauce and wonderfully soothing for scorched tongues.

*See basic recipes for corn and wheat tortillas which follow.

A selection of dried chillies, tortilla flour and some canned products can be had from:

Lourdes Nichols,
'Chimalistac', 17 Upper Hollis,
Great Missenden, Bucks., England.
Tel. 024 06 4348

Gaedke & Co.,
Mexiko-Haus, Godeffroystrasse 48,
2000 - Hamburg 55, West Germany.
Tel. 040 86 25 08

Tortillas de maíz

CORN TORTILLAS

Illustrated on pages 12 and 50–51

METRIC/IMPERIAL	AMERICAN
250 g/8 oz *tortilla* flour	2 cups *tortilla* flour
50 g/2 oz plain white flour	$\frac{1}{2}$ cup all-purpose flour
about 350 ml/12 fl oz hand-hot water	about 1$\frac{1}{2}$ cups hand-hot water

Mix together (or process using the plastic blade of a food processor) the two flours and the water (don't add any salt). Rest the dough, covered with a damp cloth, for about 30 minutes. Meanwhile, cut two 15 cm/6 inch discs from a plastic bag.

Heat a large griddle or heavy frying pan. Take a piece of dough about the size of a golf ball and roll it out thinly and evenly with a rolling pin between the two discs of plastic, rotating at each roll to get a roughly even circle of about 15 cm/6 inches in diameter and 2 mm/$\frac{1}{16}$ inch thick. Alternatively, use a tortilla press. Peel off the top plastic and transfer the tortilla from the bottom plastic on to your hand, letting about half of the tortilla hang over the outer edge of your hand. Then lay (rather than hurl) the tortilla down on the hot griddle. You should hear a slightly protesting sizzle, and in about 60 seconds the tortilla should have puffed up and be done on one side. Turn it over and cook the second side.

Put the tortilla on a cloth-lined plate or basket, cover it up and keep warm as you continue with the rest of the dough.

Tortillas will keep 4–5 days in their cloth, overwrapped in a plastic bag, in the refrigerator, and they freeze perfectly. *Makes about 24.*

NOTES

Don't worry if you don't get perfect circles with your first attempts, or if they look a bit ragged and hole-y. As with pancakes or crêpes, your first attempts are usually best fed to the dog. If your tortillas are hard and crisp rather than supple and bendy, your griddle wasn't hot enough and you dwelt too long on the whole affair: it shouldn't take more than a couple of minutes to cook both sides. Since all the recipes in which you will be using tortillas involve their being cooked again, it is better to under rather than overdo them.

Tortillas de harina

WHEAT TORTILLAS

Illustrated on pages 50–51

METRIC/IMPERIAL	AMERICAN
500 g/1 lb unbleached or plain flour	4 cups all-purpose flour
125 g/4 oz white vegetable shortening	$\frac{1}{2}$ cup shortening
2 teaspoons salt	2 teaspoons salt
250 ml/8 fl oz hand-hot water	1 cup hand-hot water

Mix together (or process using the plastic blade of a food processor) the flour, shortening and salt, as if making pastry. Add the water to make a smooth, supple dough which does not stick to your hands or working surface. Divide the dough into golf ball-sized pieces.

Heat a large griddle or heavy frying pan. Roll out one piece of dough with a lightly floured pin as thinly as you can on an unfloured pastry slab or stainless steel working top, rotating the pin (rather than the tortilla) at each roll so as to get an even circle about 15 cm/6 inches in diameter. Peel the tortilla off the working surface and lay it on the heated griddle or pan. You should hear a slightly protesting sizzle and in 60 seconds it should have puffed up and be done on one side. Flip it over, cook the other side, then stack up on a plate covered with a dish towel.

Continue in this way until all the tortillas are made. They will keep 4–5 days in their towel, overwrapped in a plastic bag, in the refrigerator, and freeze perfectly. *Makes about 30.*

NOTES

Wheat tortillas must be supple and bendy, and to achieve this you must have the griddle really hot. It's also important to work quickly: if you dwell on the whole thing too long, you will have cardboard tortillas. Don't take more than a couple of minutes to do both sides; if you are taking longer, then your heat is not enough. It is better to under rather than overdo them, since all the recipes using them require them to be heated up again or baked in a finished dish.

SOUPS

'Siete virtudes tiene la sopa: quita el hambre, sed da poca;
hace dormir, tambien digerir;
siempre agrada, nunca enfada,
y hace la cara colorada' *

Soups are a way of life for the Mexican: so much so that my attempts to convert my Mexican students of French cooking to the idea of starting a meal in any other way fell completely flat. It gradually dawned on me that to a Mexican, a meal is simply not a proper job if it doesn't start with soup. As a result, there's a wealth of recipes to choose from, all equally delicious. In my final choice, I've steered a bit of a middle course, leaving out at one end the sort of vegetable soups you can find in any book, and at the other, the rather more bizarre ones involving pigs' heads and other paraphernalia. In all the recipes, the use of a good, rich, homemade stock will about double the deliciousness of the finished article.

SOPAS	SOUPS
Sopa poblana	Pork, corn, courgette [zucchini] and avocado soup
Sopa de tortilla	Tortilla soup with tomatoes, chillies and stock
Sopa de elote roja	Tomato and corn chowder
Sopa de aguacate	Hot avocado soup
Sopa de frijól	Black bean soup
Sopa de flor de calabaza	Courgette [zucchini] flower soup
Sopa de champiñón con flor	Mushroom and courgette [zucchini] flower soup
Sopa de lentejas con plátano	Lentil soup with banana
Caldo de haba	Dried broad bean broth
Sopa de elote con chile	Corn soup with green chillies
Chilpachole de atún	Spicy tuna soup
Sopa de pescado	Fish soup
Caldo tlalpeño	Vegetable soup with shredded chicken, chick peas and chillies

*'The virtues of soup are sevenfold: it fills you up, quenches your thirst; sends you to sleep, aids the digestion; always pleases, never annoys, and gives you a nice red face!'

Sopa poblana

PORK, CORN, COURGETTE [ZUCCHINI] AND AVOCADO SOUP FROM
PUEBLA

METRIC/IMPERIAL
250 g/8 oz lean boneless pork, cut in cubes
1 tablespoon lard or oil
1 onion, peeled and finely chopped
2–3 large tomatoes (about 400 g/14 oz),
  peeled and diced
kernels from 2 corn cobs, or 350 g/12 oz
  frozen corn kernels
2 courgettes (about 250 g/8 oz), roughly
  chopped
2 fresh green chillies, finely chopped
1–1.5 litres/1¾–2½ pints stock
salt and pepper
2 avocados
lime or lemon juice
50 g/2 oz Cheddar cheese, grated
lime or lemon wedges to serve

AMERICAN
½ lb lean boneless pork, cut into cubes
1 tablespoon lard or oil
1 onion, peeled and finely chopped
2–3 large tomatoes (about 14 oz), peeled
  and diced
kernels from 2 ears of corn, or ¾ lb (about
  2¼ cups) frozen whole kernel corn
2 zucchini (about ½ lb), roughly chopped
2 fresh green chilies, finely chopped
1–1½ quarts stock
salt and pepper
2 avocados
lime or lemon juice
½ cup grated Cheddar cheese
lime or lemon wedges for serving

Brown the pork pieces in the lard or oil over moderately high heat. Add the
onion and cook till soft. Stir in the tomatoes and fry till the juice runs. Add the
corn kernels, courgettes [zucchini] and chillies and cook, stirring, until a nice
thick paste is formed. Moisten with the stock and simmer for 15–20 minutes or
until the vegetables are barely cooked. Season to taste (always add salt to
corn only at the end, otherwise you'll toughen it).

Peel the avocados, taking care not to squash or bruise them. Divide into
eight segments. Sprinkle with lime or lemon juice to prevent discoloration
and arrange them on top of the soup. Sprinkle on the cheese and serve lime or
lemon wedges on the side for each person to squeeze on the soup at will.

Sopa de tortilla

TORTILLA SOUP WITH TOMATOES, CHILLIES AND STOCK

Illustrated on page 29

METRIC/IMPERIAL
8 stale tortillas, cut in thin strips
oil or lard to a depth of about 5 mm/¼ inch
1 onion, peeled
2 large tomatoes (about 350 g/12 oz), or 1
  400-g/14-oz can peeled tomatoes
2 fresh green chillies
1 clove garlic
salt
1.5 litres/2½ pints best chicken stock
chopped fresh *epazote* or coriander
  (optional)
grated Cheddar or Parmesan cheese
2 *chiles pasilla*, fried, to garnish (optional)

AMERICAN
8 stale tortillas, cut into thin strips
oil or lard to a depth of about ¼ inch
1 onion, peeled
2 large tomatoes (about ¾ lb), or 1 16-oz
  can peeled tomatoes
2 fresh green chilies
1 clove garlic
salt
1½ quarts best chicken stock
chopped fresh *epazote* or coriander
  (optional)
grated Cheddar or Parmesan cheese
2 *chiles pasilla*, fried, for garnish (optional)

In a large, heavy saucepan, fry the tortilla strips in the oil or lard until lightly golden. Drain on paper towels. Pour off all but about 1 tablespoon fat and set the pan aside.

Put the onion, fresh tomatoes (not canned ones), chillies and garlic on a foil-lined baking sheet (helps reduce mess) and grill [broil] until lightly blistered and soft. Chop the onion and tomatoes roughly (don't skin the tomatoes – the flavour is in the toasted bits). Remove seeds and stalks from the chillies. Slip the garlic out of its jacket. Place the vegetables in the container of a food processor or blender (add the canned tomatoes now, with their juice) and blend all together with salt to taste.

Reheat the fat in the saucepan to almost smoking, throw in the vegetable purée and fry well, stirring all around till thick and syrupy. Add the stock and herbs, if used, bring back to the boil and simmer for 20 minutes.

Add the fried tortilla strips and simmer for a further 5 minutes or so – don't overdo it; the tortillas should retain a bit of crispness.

To serve, sprinkle with grated cheese and garnish with the (optional but traditional) fried *chiles pasilla*, which are purely for show and should on no account be eaten!

Sopa de elote roja

TOMATO AND CORN CHOWDER

METRIC/IMPERIAL	AMERICAN
1 onion, peeled and chopped	1 onion, peeled and chopped
1 clove garlic, peeled and crushed	1 clove garlic, peeled and minced
1 tablespoon lard or oil	1 tablespoon lard or oil
3 large tomatoes (about 500 g/1 lb), peeled, seeded and chopped, or 1 400-g/14-oz can peeled tomatoes	3 large tomatoes (about 1 lb), peeled, seeded and chopped, or 1 16-oz can peeled tomatoes
1.5 litres/2½ pints chicken stock	1½ quarts chicken stock
kernels from 3 corn cobs, or about 500 g/1 lb frozen corn kernels	kernels from 3 ears of corn, or 1 lb (about 3 cups) frozen whole kernel corn
salt and pepper	salt and pepper
6 slices quick-melting cheese or cream cheese	6 slices quick-melting cheese or cream cheese
Tabasco sauce (optional)	hot pepper sauce (optional)

Soften the onion and garlic in the lard or oil without browning. Add the tomatoes, cover and cook 10 minutes to evaporate and concentrate the juices.

Add the stock and bring to the boil, then add the corn kernels and simmer for about 10 minutes or until just tender. The soup can then either be blended in a food processor or blender to the desired consistency or left rough. Season to taste (don't add salt till now or you risk toughening the corn).

Reheat gently and serve piping hot with a slice of cheese on each portion, and a dash of optional Tabasco sauce to give it a bit of final bite.

Sopa de aguacate

HOT AVOCADO SOUP

Illustrated on page 29

METRIC/IMPERIAL
1 tablespoon finely chopped onion
1 small clove garlic, peeled and crushed
1–2 fresh green chillies, seeded and very
  finely chopped
1 teaspoon oil
1.5 litres/2½ pints very best chicken stock
1 tablespoon chopped fresh coriander
salt and pepper
2 avocados, peeled and stoned
juice of 1 lime
a few cooked peeled prawns or crispy-fried
  tortilla strips to garnish

AMERICAN
1 tablespoon finely minced onion
1 small clove garlic, peeled and minced
1–2 fresh green chilies, seeded and very
  finely chopped
1 teaspoon oil
1½ quarts very best chicken stock
1 tablespoon chopped fresh coriander
salt and pepper
2 avocados, peeled and seeded
juice of 1 lime
a few cooked, shelled and deveined shrimp
  or crispy-fried tortilla strips for garnish

Soften the onion, garlic and chilli in the oil without browning. Moisten with the stock, add the coriander and season carefully. Simmer for 10 minutes. Remove from the heat.

Place the avocados in the container of a food processor or blender with a little of the hot stock and the lime juice and blend until smooth. Pour into the saucepan, whisking well to blend, and heat through gently. On no account allow the soup to boil or it will be bitter. Garnish with prawns [shrimp] (elegant) or tortilla strips (friendly).

Sopa de frijól

BLACK BEAN SOUP

Don't soak your beans before cooking, whatever anyone tells you. It's not only unnecessary, but you lose a lot of their flavour and goodness, especially if you throw away the soaking water.

METRIC/IMPERIAL
250 g/8 oz dried black beans
1.5 litres/2½ pints cold water
fresh *epazote* leaves (optional)
2 tablespoons lard
2 onions, peeled and 1 chopped
1 clove garlic, peeled
1 large tomato (about 150 g/5 oz), peeled
  and chopped
1 fresh green chilli, finely chopped
salt
sour cream
grated Parmesan cheese
chopped fresh *epazote* leaves or crumbled
  oregano to garnish

AMERICAN
½ lb (about 1 cup) dried black beans
1½ quarts cold water
fresh *epazote* leaves (optional)
2 tablespoons lard
2 onions, peeled and 1 chopped
1 clove garlic, peeled
1 large tomato (about 5 oz), peeled and
  chopped
1 fresh green chili, finely chopped
salt
sour cream
grated Parmesan cheese
chopped fresh *epazote* leaves or crumbled
  oregano for garnish

Place the beans in a saucepan and cover with the water. Add the *epazote*, 1 tablespoon of the lard, the whole onion and the garlic and simmer for $1\frac{1}{2}$–2 hours or until the beans are barely tender.

Lift out a spoonful of beans and blow on them; the skin should break open and retract a little. In a heavy frying pan next to your bean pan, fry the chopped onion in the remaining lard until golden brown. Add the tomato and chilli and cook, stirring, until thick. Ladle in a good dollop of beans plus their liquid, and continue to cook, stirring and mashing with a wooden spoon, until really thick and syrupy.

Pour the mixture back into the bean pot, and add salt to taste (like corn, add salt to beans only at the end of their cooking time, or you'll toughen the skins). Continue cooking until the beans are quite tender (about 30 minutes more, but it won't hurt them if you leave them longer). You can then either blend the soup in a food processor or blender, or leave it all beany and soupy.

To serve, top with a dollop of sour cream, some cheese and the herbs. A fried egg on top of each serving makes the soup into a substantial, protein-rich, high-fibre supper.

Sopa de flor de calabaza

COURGETTE [ZUCCHINI] FLOWER SOUP

If you can't quite muster the required 30 or 40 flowers needed from your own veggie patch, go and raid your neighbour's: this is a memorable soup and well worth the effort and possible unpopularity – especially if you invite him to join you at the feast.

METRIC/IMPERIAL	AMERICAN
30–40 courgette flowers (see Glossary)	30–40 zucchini flowers (see Glossary)
1 medium onion, peeled and chopped	1 medium-size onion, peeled and chopped
1 tablespoon oil or lard	1 tablespoon oil or lard
2 large tomatoes (about 350 g/12 oz), peeled and chopped	2 large tomatoes (about $\frac{3}{4}$ lb), peeled and chopped
chopped fresh *epazote* (optional)	chopped fresh *epazote* (optional)
salt and pepper	salt and pepper
1.5–2 litres/$2\frac{1}{2}$–$3\frac{1}{2}$ pints best chicken stock	$1\frac{1}{2}$–2 quarts best chicken stock
sour cream to serve	sour cream for serving

Pull off the spiky bits from around the outside of the flower base and separate the flowers from the stalks. Set aside 6 of the most beautiful flowers for the garnish. Chop the remaining flowers roughly and set aside. Strip the stalks as if peeling celery and chop roughly.

Soften the stalks with the onion in the oil or lard without browning, then add the tomatoes and cook, stirring, till thick and somewhat reduced. Add the roughly chopped flowers, herbs, and salt and pepper to taste. Moisten with the stock and simmer for about 20 minutes – no more as the flowers are very delicate and don't need much cooking.

Pour into the container of a food processor or blender and blend smooth. Garnish with the whole reserved flowers and splodges of sour cream.

Sopa de champiñón con flor

MUSHROOM AND COURGETTE [ZUCCHINI] FLOWER SOUP

Courgette [zucchini] flowers have a most delicate and delicious flavour which can all too easily be overpowered; here the mushrooms complement and enhance without dominating.

METRIC/IMPERIAL	AMERICAN
about 40 courgette flowers (see Glossary)	about 40 zucchini flowers (see Glossary)
1 small onion, peeled and finely chopped	1 small onion, peeled and finely chopped
1 teaspoon oil	1 teaspoon oil
25g/1oz butter	2 tablespoons butter
250g/8oz mushrooms, thinly sliced	$\frac{1}{2}$lb mushrooms, thinly sliced
salt and pepper	salt and pepper
1.5 litres/2$\frac{1}{2}$ pints best chicken stock	1$\frac{1}{2}$ quarts best chicken stock
250–500ml/8–16floz milk or single cream	1–2 cups milk or light cream

Pull off the spiky bits from around the outside of the flower base and separate the flowers from the stalks. Set aside 6 of the most beautiful flowers for the garnish. Chop the remaining flowers roughly and set aside. Strip the stringy outside part off the stalks, as if you were peeling stringy celery, and chop finely.

Soften the stalks with the onion in the oil and butter without browning, then add mushrooms and chopped flowers. Season lightly, cover and cook for 5 minutes or until the juices are rendered. Raise the heat and fry, uncovered, stirring until the juices evaporate. Add the stock and simmer for 10–15 minutes more.

The flowers will thicken the soup quite a lot, so add enough milk or cream at the end to thin it down as necessary and simmer a further 5 minutes. Adjust the seasoning. Float a reserved flower on top of each portion and serve immediately.

Sopa de lentejas con plátano

LENTIL SOUP WITH BANANA

METRIC/IMPERIAL	AMERICAN
250g/8oz brown lentils	1 cup brown lentils
1 litre/1$\frac{3}{4}$ pints water	1 quart water
1 small onion, peeled	1 small onion, peeled
1 clove garlic, peeled	1 clove garlic, peeled
salt and pepper	salt and pepper
2 large tomatoes (about 350g/12oz)	2 large tomatoes (about $\frac{3}{4}$lb)
1 tablespoon lard	1 tablespoon lard
1 banana	1 banana
chopped parsley	chopped parsley
Tabasco sauce to taste	hot pepper sauce to taste

Cover the lentils with the water, add the onion, garlic, and salt and pepper to taste and simmer until soft (about 30 minutes).

Grill [broil] the tomatoes until blistered and soft. Retrieve the onion and garlic from the lentil pot and purée together with the tomatoes in a food processor or blender until smooth.

In a large heavy saucepan, heat the lard till almost smoking. Throw in the purée and fry hard, stirring, till thick and tasty, and somewhat reduced. Pour on the lentils and their broth, stir well and simmer a further 10 minutes or so or until the flavours are blended.

Peel the banana and slice thickly on the slant. Add to the soup for the last 5 minutes of cooking. Just before serving, sprinkle with chopped parsley, and several splashes of Tabasco sauce to smarten it up a bit.

Caldo de haba

DRIED BROAD BEAN BROTH

For some reason, this is typically a Lenten soup. It's certainly no penance to eat it, but then I've never really understood the principle of fasting . . . Italian shops keep dried broad beans, but be sure they are the peeled ones, or you're in a mess.

METRIC/IMPERIAL
350 g/12 oz dried peeled broad beans
1 onion, peeled and chopped
2 cloves garlic, peeled and chopped
1 tablespoon lard
2 large tomatoes (about 350 g/12 oz), peeled and chopped
1.5 litres/2½ pints water or ham stock
4 tablespoons chopped fresh coriander
1 sprig fresh mint
salt and pepper
2 *chiles pasilla*, fried, or several dashes of Tabasco sauce (optional)
crumbly white cheese to garnish

AMERICAN
¾ lb dried broad or fava beans (about 1¾ cups)
1 onion, peeled and chopped
2 cloves garlic, peeled and chopped
1 tablespoon lard
2 large tomatoes (about ¾ lb), peeled and chopped
1½ quarts water or ham stock
¼ cup chopped fresh coriander
1 sprig fresh mint
salt and pepper
2 *chiles pasilla*, fried, or several dashes of hot pepper sauce (optional)
crumbly white cheese for garnish

Fry the beans with the onion and garlic in the hot lard, stirring, until evenly golden. Add the tomatoes and cook until somewhat reduced. Moisten with the water or stock, add the herbs, salt and pepper to taste and simmer for 1½–2 hours, or until the beans are tender (depends on how ancient your beans are).

Garnish with the fried *chiles* (don't let anyone eat them) or Tabasco sauce, more chopped coriander if you have it, and a good crumble of cheese. A wonderful, earthy, peasant affair.

Sopa de elote con chile

CORN SOUP WITH GREEN CHILLIES

Illustrated on page 29

METRIC/IMPERIAL	AMERICAN
2–3 fresh green chillies, seeded and cut in strips	2–3 fresh green chilies, seeded and cut in strips
1 onion, peeled and chopped	1 onion, peeled and chopped
1 tablespoon oil	1 tablespoon oil
kernels from 3 corn cobs, or 500 g/1 lb frozen corn kernels	kernels from 3 ears of corn, or 1 lb (about 3 cups) frozen whole kernel corn
1 litre/1¾ pints chicken stock	1 quart chicken stock
500 ml/16 fl oz milk	2 cups milk
salt	salt
sour cream or *crème fraiche*	chopped fresh *epazote* (optional)
chopped fresh *epazote* (optional)	sour cream or *crème fraiche*

Soften the prepared chillies with the onion in the oil without browning, then add the corn kernels, stock and milk and simmer until just tender (about 10 minutes). Add salt to taste and simmer 5 minutes more.

Cool a little, then pour into the container of a food processor or blender and blend to the desired consistency. Garnish with cream and the *epazote*, if used, and serve piping hot.

Chilpachole de atún

SPICY TUNA SOUP

METRIC/IMPERIAL	AMERICAN
2 large tomatoes (about 350 g/12 oz)	2 large tomatoes (about ¾ lb)
2 fresh red or green chillies	2 fresh red or green chilies
1 onion, peeled	1 onion, peeled
2 cloves garlic	2 cloves garlic
1 tablespoon olive oil	1 tablespoon olive oil
1.5 litres/2½ pints fish or chicken stock or water	1½ quarts fish or chicken stock or water
juice of 1 lime	juice of 1 lime
300 g/10 oz canned tuna fish, drained and mashed	10 oz canned tuna fish, drained and mashed (about 1 cup)
chopped fresh *epazote* (optional)	chopped fresh *epazote* (optional)
salt	salt

Grill [broil] the tomatoes, chillies, onion and garlic until blistered and soft. Quarter the tomatoes and onion; peel the garlic; seed the chillies and remove the stalks. Place the vegetables in the container of a food processor or blender and blend to a smooth purée.

Heat the oil in a large heavy saucepan, throw in the purée and cook hard, stirring, until well-reduced and full of flavour. Add the stock or water, lime juice, tuna, herbs, if used, and salt to taste and bring back to the boil. Simmer for about 20 minutes, or until rich and tasty. The soup can be blended smooth or left rough.

Sopa de pescado

FISH SOUP

This evokes memories of shimmering days by the Pacific where lunch was inevitably taken on hard, wicker chairs under faded, palm-thatched parasols. Soup was always on the menu, in spite of the heat, always delicious and surprisingly refreshing – in the same way, I suppose, that a hot cup of tea is thirst-quenching on even the hottest day.

METRIC/IMPERIAL	AMERICAN
3 large tomatoes (about 500 g/1 lb)	3 large tomatoes (about 1 lb)
2 cloves garlic	2 cloves garlic
2–3 tablespoons olive oil	2–3 tablespoons olive oil
2 medium onions (about 125 g/4 oz), peeled and chopped	2 medium-size onions (about $\frac{1}{4}$ lb), peeled and chopped
2 leeks, white part only, chopped	2 leeks, white part only, chopped
1 bouquet garni (parsley, thyme and bay leaf)	1 bouquet garni (parsley, thyme and bay leaf)
about 1 kg/2 lb fish trimmings (heads, bones etc.)	about 2 lb fish trimmings (heads, bones, etc.)
about 1.5 litres/2$\frac{1}{2}$ pints water	about 1$\frac{1}{2}$ quarts water
300 ml/$\frac{1}{2}$ pint dry white wine	1$\frac{1}{4}$ cups dry white wine
juice of 1 lime	juice of 1 lime
2 fresh or canned green chillies	2 fresh or canned green chilies
salt	salt
350 g/12 oz fresh fish fillets or shellfish, cut in cubes	$\frac{3}{4}$ lb fresh fish fillets or shellfish, cut into cubes
tortilla strips to garnish	tortilla strips for garnish
lime wedges to serve	lime wedges for serving

Grill [broil] the tomatoes and garlic till soft and blistered. Peel the garlic, then blend smooth with the tomatoes.

Heat the oil in a saucepan and fry the onions and leeks till soft. Add the blended tomatoes and bouquet garni, and cook for 5–10 minutes or until thick and tasty. Add the fish trimmings and barely cover with water. Add the wine, lime juice, chillies (don't puncture, unless you want your soup extremely spicy) and salt to taste. Simmer for 30 minutes or until really rich and tasty.

Strain into a large bowl, pressing down on the vegetables and bones to extract maximum flavour. Return the stock to the pan and add the fish or shellfish. Simmer for a further 10–15 minutes or until the fish or seafood is just cooked.

Garnish with tortilla strips and serve with lime wedges for each guest to squeeze on.

Caldo tlalpeño

VEGETABLE SOUP WITH SHREDDED CHICKEN, CHICK PEAS AND
CHILLIES

Tlalpan, where this soup comes from, is a southern suburb of Mexico City
which caters, among other things, for the Sunday brunch enthusiast – whole
streets are lined with appetizing little stands selling tempting bowls and
plates of this and that, and the *mariachi* bands in the restaurants reach a
mounting crescendo as they move from table to table – and all at 11 o'clock on
a Sunday morning . . .

METRIC/IMPERIAL
2 skinless, boneless chicken breasts or
  turkey escalopes (about 250 g/8 oz)
1.5 litres/2½ pints chicken stock
salt and pepper
1 onion, peeled and chopped
1 clove garlic, peeled and crushed
1 tablespoon lard
2 large tomatoes (about 350 g/12 oz), peeled
  and chopped
250 g/8 oz French beans
2 medium carrots, peeled and cut in strips
1 227-g/8-oz can chick peas, drained, or
  250 g/8 oz cooked chick peas
2 *chiles chipotles*, dried or canned
  (optional)
chopped fresh coriander or mint
1 avocado, peeled, stoned and cut in 8
  strips
lime wedges to serve

AMERICAN
2 skinless, boneless chicken breast halves
  or 2 turkey cutlets (about ½ lb)
1½ quarts chicken stock
salt and pepper
1 onion, peeled and chopped
1 clove garlic, peeled and minced
1 tablespoon lard
2 large tomatoes (about ¾ lb), peeled and
  chopped
½ lb green beans
2 medium-size carrots, peeled and cut into
  strips
1 cup canned or cooked chick peas
  (garbanzos), drained
2 *chiles chipotles*, dried or canned
  (optional)
chopped fresh coriander or mint
1 avocado, peeled, seeded and cut into 8
  slices
lime wedges for serving

Simmer the chicken or turkey in the stock with salt and pepper to taste until
just tender. Drain, reserving the stock. Shred the meat with fingers or forks
into thin strips. Set aside.

In a large, heavy pan or flameproof casserole, soften the onion and garlic in
the lard without browning. Add the tomatoes and cook, stirring, till well-
reduced and syrupy. Add the reserved stock and bring to the boil. Throw in
the beans, carrots, chick peas, *chiles*, if used, and herbs and simmer 20–30
minutes or until well-flavoured. (Of course you may have to skip the *chiles*,
but it's a pity, as their unique smokey flavour – they're the only smoked, dried
chilli – really gives the soup an extra something.)

Garnish with avocado slices and serve with lime wedges to squeeze on in
the regulation manner.

Right from the top: *sopa de elote con chile* (page 26), *sopa de tortilla* (page 20),
sopa de aguacate (page 22)
Overleaf clockwise from left: *tostadas* (pages 46–7), *ensalada de Nochebuena* (page
41), *ensalada de calabacita y ejote* (page 42)

SAUCES AND DIPS

Mexican sauces are arrived at, in the main, by gently toasting on griddle or grill [broiler] the main protagonists in the drama (chillies, tomato, onion, garlic, spices), then blending until of the desired consistency. In the old days, of course, all sauces would be ground in a *molcajete*, or pestle and mortar made of rough volcanic stone (see notes on special equipment in the Introduction), but on the whole a blender or food processor does a pretty good job. I would, however, make an exception in the case of that best-known and most widely travelled of Mexican sauces, *guacamole*, preferring always to make it in the *molcajete*.

All of these sauces are used as table sauces to accompany plainly cooked meats, fish or eggs: in this way, you can add just the degree of heat which suits you, rather in the same way that we would serve mustard or chutney on the table. Some sauces (especially *guacamole*) can be used as dips, served with tortilla or potato crisps [chips]. Also included is a basic tomato sauce, summer and winter versions, with fairly detailed instructions, for while I know it's irritating to be referred back all the time in a cookery book to page so-&-so, this sauce is one which comes up often in other recipes. Also, the method for making it serves as a model for all Mexican sauces, which appear in even greater variety in the meat and fish chapters.

Guacamole	Avocado sauce
Salsa mexicana	Uncooked tomato sauce
Salsa de chiles rojos	Red chilli sauce
Salsa verde	Sharp green tomato or gooseberry sauce
Caldillo de jitomate	Basic tomato sauce
de verano	summer version
de invierno	winter version

Left *cebiche* (page 39)

Guacamole

AVOCADO SAUCE

Illustrated on page 49

It's interesting to note that *mo-le* (the accent is on the first syllable) means simply a sauce and comes from the Nahuatl word *molli*, meaning concoction or mixture. Hence, *guaca-mole* is a concoction made from *aguaca-tes* – avocados. As previously mentioned, this is the one sauce which should really be made in a pestle and mortar since you get about half the flavour out of your chillies, coriander and avocados if you just whizz them up into a sort of baby-food affair in your food processor or blender. My own *molcajete* went everywhere with us on our travels around Mexico, and no picnic was complete without lashings of freshly-made *guacamole*, its palest green contrasting sharply with the darkest black volcanic stone of the *molcajete* – and always the avocado stones plumped on top, since tradition has it that they prevent the sauce from discolouring. Guacamole goes beautifully with just about anything, and there's never *quite* enough . . .

METRIC/IMPERIAL	AMERICAN
1 small clove garlic, peeled	1 small clove garlic, peeled
handful of fresh coriander leaves	handful of fresh coriander leaves
1–2 small fresh green chillies	1–2 small fresh green chilies
½ teaspoon salt	½ teaspoon salt
2 large ripe avocados, peeled and stoned (stones reserved)	2 large ripe avocados, peeled and seeded (seeds reserved)
juice of 1 lime	juice of 1 lime
2–3 tablespoons water	2–3 tablespoons water
finely chopped onion and/or diced tomato (optional)	finely chopped onion and/or diced tomato (optional)

Reduce the garlic, coriander leaves and chillies to a paste with the salt in your *molcajete*. Mash in the avocados, then add the lime juice and enough water to make a dropping consistency. Stir in the onion and tomato, if used, at the end and bury the avocado stones in the sauce. Serve straight from the *molcajete* or in a nice rustic little bowl. *Makes about 250ml/8 fl oz.*

Salsa mexicana

UNCOOKED TOMATO SAUCE

Illustrated on page 69

A patriotic one, this, with all three colours of the Mexican flag supposedly represented by the red, white and green of the ingredients – tomatoes, onion, coriander and chillies. *Salsa mexicana* goes with *quesadillas, tacos, burritos* or any barbecued or grilled [broiled] meat or fish.

METRIC/IMPERIAL	AMERICAN
1 large tomato (about 150 g/5 oz), diced	1 large tomato (about 5 oz), diced
1 tablespoon finely chopped onion	1 tablespoon finely chopped onion
1–2 fresh green chillies, seeded and finely chopped	1–2 fresh green chillies, seeded and finely chopped
handful of fresh coriander leaves, finely chopped	handful of fresh coriander leaves, finely chopped
1 teaspoon salt	1 teaspoon salt
little lime juice (optional)	little lime juice (optional)

Stir all the ingredients gently together and serve in a nice little bowl. Don't make up the sauce more than an hour before you plan to serve it, otherwise the tomatoes will go all weepy and the sauce will lose its bite. *Makes about 250 ml/8 fl oz.*

Salsa de chiles rojos

RED CHILLI SAUCE

The red, or ripened, chillies have plenty of bite, as well as an interesting sort of sweetness not to be found when in their green state. This sauce goes particularly well with all egg dishes, for brunch.

METRIC/IMPERIAL	AMERICAN
6 fresh red chillies, seeded and cut into fine strips	6 fresh red chilies, seeded and cut into fine strips
3 large tomatoes (about 500 g/1 lb)	3 large tomatoes (about 1 lb)
2 cloves garlic, peeled and chopped	2 cloves garlic, peeled and chopped
1 small onion, peeled and chopped	1 small onion, peeled and chopped
1 tablespoon oil or lard	1 tablespoon oil or lard
salt	salt

Soak the chillies in cold salted water, changing the water several times if you feel the chillies are very hot (i.e. if your eyes are watering, your finger-ends smarting and everyone around you coughing and spluttering).

Meanwhile, grill [broil] the tomatoes until blistered and soft, then place – skins and all – in a food processor or blender with the garlic and onion. Blend until smooth.

Heat the oil or lard to almost smoking, throw in the tomato mixture and cook, stirring, until syrupy and thick. Add the drained chilli strips and salt to taste, and cook gently for a further 10–15 minutes.

Serve hot, and if using as a table sauce, keep warm on a spirit burner. *Makes about 500 ml/17 fl oz.*

Salsa verde

SHARP GREEN TOMATO OR GOOSEBERRY SAUCE

As mentioned in the Glossary, Mexicans make great use of the green tomato or *Physalis edulis*. It is sadly deficient elsewhere, but is beginning to creep in, in cans mainly, and in some cases in the vegetable plots of fanatic Mexicophiles. I have had correspondence with a delightful-sounding gentleman in the depths of inner Switzerland who grows green tomatoes with great success on his balcony. However, don't dismay, since the main point of the green tomato is its sharp acidity to provide a contrast to rich dishes (notably pork) and green gooseberries make a very acceptable sustitute. I have even used sorrel with quite convincing results. The sauce goes very well with *tacos* and *burritos*, and with any grilled [broiled] fish.

METRIC/IMPERIAL
1 15-oz/425-g can Mexican green tomatoes, drained, or 350 g/12 oz green gooseberries, topped and tailed, or 350 g/12 oz fresh Mexican green tomatoes from your garden (about 20), husks removed
2 fresh green chillies
1 small onion, peeled and chopped
1 clove garlic, peeled and chopped
handful of fresh coriander
salt

AMERICAN
1 16-oz can Mexican green tomatoes, drained, or $\frac{3}{4}$ lb green gooseberries, trimmed, or $\frac{3}{4}$ lb fresh Mexican green tomatoes from your garden (about 20), husks removed
2 fresh green chilies
1 small onion, peeled and chopped
1 clove garlic, peeled and chopped
handful of fresh coriander leaves
salt

If using fresh green tomatoes or gooseberries, place them in a saucepan with the chillies, barely cover with water and simmer until just soft, but not bursting out all over the place (about 15 minutes). Cool in the cooking liquid.

Pour the mixture into a food processor or blender (if using canned tomatoes, they come in here) and add the onion, garlic, coriander, and salt to taste. Blend until smooth. Serve cold. *Makes about 500 ml/17 fl oz.*

Caldillo de jitomate

BASIC TOMATO SAUCE (SUMMER)

Both these tomato sauces freeze well, so it makes particularly good sense to buy or pick lots of tomatoes at the end of the summer when there's a glut and make up a big quantity. Use tomato sauce in all manner of Mexican dishes: fried or scrambled eggs, with pork dishes, barbecued meats, over stuffed chillies/peppers, with *tacos* and *burritos*, *enchiladas*, Aztec pie . . . you name it, and it'll go.

METRIC/IMPERIAL	AMERICAN
4 large tomatoes (about 675 g/1½ lb)	4 large tomatoes (about 1½ lb)
2 fresh green chillies	2 fresh green chillies
1 clove garlic	1 clove garlic
1 small onion, peeled	1 small onion, peeled
1 teaspoon salt	1 teaspoon salt
1 tablespoon lard or oil	1 tablespoon lard or oil
pinch of ground cinnamon or aniseed (optional)	pinch of ground cinnamon or aniseed (optional)

Place the tomatoes, chillies, garlic and onion on a baking sheet lined with foil (helps reduce mess) or onto a foil-lined grill [broiler] pan. Grill [broil] until lightly blistered and soft. Slip the garlic out of its jacket and into the container of a food processor or blender. Cut the stalks off the chillies and seed them; add to the processor. Quarter the tomatoes (don't peel them unless there are some really blackened patches – all the flavour and goodness is in the skin) and onion and add to the processor with the salt. Blend until quite smooth

Heat the lard or oil in a heavy, deep frying pan or saucepan (the sauce will splatter so you need a deep pan) until almost smoking or until a drop or two of purée thrown in will fizzle quite fiercely. Throw in all the purée at once (don't lose your nerve halfway through: once the whole of the bottom of the pan is covered, things will improve) and cook, stirring all over the bottom of the pan.

Add the spices, if used. Reduce the heat a bit, cover with a splatter shield and let the sauce cook steadily for 15–20 minutes, stirring from time to time, until rich and thick. *Makes about 500 ml/17 fl oz.*

BASIC TOMATO SAUCE (WINTER)

METRIC/IMPERIAL	AMERICAN
2 fresh green chillies, or 2 canned *chiles jalapeños en escabeche*, or 2–3 *chiles pequín* (little red dried ones, the sort you find in pickling spice)	2 fresh green chillies, or 2 canned *chiles jalapeños en escabeche*, or 2–3 *chiles pequín* (little red dried ones, the sort you find in pickling spices)
1 clove garlic	1 clove garlic
1 small onion, peeled	1 small onion, peeled
2 400-g/14-oz cans peeled plum tomatoes	2 16-oz cans peeled tomatoes
salt	salt
lard or oil	lard or oil

Grill the fresh chillies, garlic and onion until blistered and soft. Seed the chillies and remove stalks. Peel the garlic and quarter the onion. Place all these ingredients in the container of a food processor or blender, add the canned tomatoes and canned or dried chillies, if used, and salt to taste. Fry in the hot lard or oil as before, and simmer until thick. *Makes about 500 ml/17 fl oz.*

APPETIZERS

As previously mentioned, the only real way to start a meal in Mexico is with soup. However, for those of us barbarians who feel that soup doesn't invariably fit the bill, here are some dishes which might, in the true context of a Mexican meal, be served as a separate vegetable course or *antojito* after the main course, but which to my mind and to our appetites do better standing on their own as appetizers.

COLD

Cebiche	Marinated fish salad
Ensalada tricolor	Corn, avocado and pomegranate salad
Ensalada de coliflor	Cauliflower masked with *guacamole*
Ensalada de Nochebuena	Beetroot, fruit and nut salad
Ensalada de calabacita y ejote	Courgette [zucchini] and bean salad
Chiles rellenos en frío	Marinated stuffed peppers, with various fillings:
de guacamole	avocado
de frijól	bean and sardine
de papa con aguacate	potato and avocado
Tostadas	Crispy tortillas, with various toppings:
frijól con pollo	bean and chicken
guacamole	avocado
papa con chorizo	potato and sausage
papa con sardina	potato and sardine

HOT

Chiles rellenos calientes	Hot stuffed peppers, with various fillings:
de mariscos	shellfish
de elote	corn
de queso	cheese
Quesadillas	Tortilla turnovers, with various fillings:
de hongo	mushroom
de flor	courgette [zucchini] flower
de queso	cheese
de frijól	bean and tomato
de papa con chorizo	potato and sausage
Crepas con salsa de nuez	Chicken crêpes with creamy *chipotle* and walnut sauce
Crepas de flor	Crépes stuffed with courgette [zucchini] flowers

Cebiche

MARINATED FISH SALAD

Illustrated on page 32

This is one of the most widely travelled of Mexican dishes, but one which, like the game of Chinese whispers or Telephone, has lost a little in the telling. In Mexico, *sierra* (mackerel) is always used. If you can't get good, fresh mackerel, then use a firm white fish; don't go for anything fancy, since this is a simple, fresh fish salad and it's silly to pay the earth for something exotic when after 'cooking' the fish in lime juice, no-one could tell you what it was anyway. The only thing that's important is that it should be perfectly fresh. Ideally, fillet the fish yourself and use the trimmings to make a *sopa de pescado* (see page 27).

METRIC/IMPERIAL
500 g/1 lb fillets of mackerel or firm white fish (e.g. dab, plaice, hake, etc.), skinned and cubed
juice of 3 limes (about 120 ml/4 fl oz)
6 tablespoons oil
3 tablespoons tomato ketchup
½ teaspoon dried oregano or 1 tablespoon freshly chopped coriander
Worcestershire sauce
salt and pepper
2 medium tomatoes (about 250 g/8 oz), chopped
2 tablespoons very finely chopped onion
1–2 small fresh green chillies, very finely chopped
12 green olives, stoned
crisp lettuce leaves to serve
1 avocado, peeled, stoned and cubed

AMERICAN
1 lb fillets of mackerel or firm, white fish (e.g. flounder, dab, hake, etc.), skinned and cubed
juice of 3 limes (about ½ cup)
6 tablespoons oil
3 tablespoons tomato ketchup
½ teaspoon dried oregano or 1 tablespoon freshly chopped coriander
Worcestershire sauce
salt and pepper
2 medium-size tomatoes (about ½ lb), chopped
2 tablespoons very finely chopped onion
1–2 small fresh green chilies, very finely chopped
12 green olives, pitted
crisp lettuce leaves for serving
1 avocado, peeled, seeded and cubed

Marinate the fish cubes in the lime juice in a glass bowl or any non-metal container for at least 6 hours or overnight until opaque.

Drain the fish in a strainer placed over a bowl. Add to the drained juices the oil, ketchup, oregano or coriander, and Worcestershire sauce, salt and pepper to taste, whisking well as if making a vinaigrette. Mix the fish pieces with the tomatoes, onion, chillies and olives, then pour over the vinaigrette, turning to mix well.

Arrange the lettuce leaves on a shallow serving dish or on individual plates. Put the *cebiche* on top and garnish with the avocado pieces. Serve with crisp savoury biscuits [crackers] or Melba toast.

Ensalada tricolor

CORN, AVOCADO AND POMEGRANATE SALAD

Another of those patriotic jobs, this has the three colours of the Mexican flag supposedly represented by the red, white and green of its component parts. It makes a delicious, colourful and refreshing salad with just the right combination of smoothness and crunch.

METRIC/IMPERIAL	AMERICAN
3 fresh corn cobs, or about 500 g/1 lb frozen corn kernels	3 ears of corn, or 1 lb (about 3 cups) frozen whole kernel corn
salt	salt
about 150 ml/¼ pint sharp vinaigrette*	about ¾ cup sharp vinaigrette*
seeds from 2 pomegranates	seeds from 2 pomegranates
1 quantity *guacamole* (see page 34)	1 quantity *guacamole* (see page 34)

Cook the fresh corn in boiling water for about 10 minutes or until just tender. (Cook frozen corn according to the packet directions.) Drain and refresh under cold running water, then pare off the kernels. Season well with salt (don't add salt to the cooking water or you'll toughen the corn), and pour on the vinaigrette while still warm. Toss to coat and allow to cool.

When ready to serve, arrange the corn salad in the middle of a nice, round dish. Surround with the pomegranate seeds and place an outer ring of guacamole around the edge.

*If you don't have a favourite recipe for this, use the dressing in *ensalada de Nochebuena*, page 41.

Ensalada de coliflor

CAULIFLOWER MASKED WITH GUACAMOLE

This unusual salad of crisp-cooked cauliflowerets served with an avocado dressing is surprisingly delicious. The addition of aniseed to the cauliflower cooking water gives it a pleasant flavour. Be sure not to overdo the cooking time – the cauliflower should retain more than a suspicion of crunch.

METRIC/IMPERIAL	AMERICAN
1 medium cauliflower, broken into flowerets	1 medium-size cauliflower, broken into flowerets
salt	salt
pinch of aniseed or fennel seeds	pinch of aniseed or fennel seeds
1 quantity *guacamole* (see page 34)	1 quantity *guacamole* (see page 34)
1 medium tomato, chopped	1 medium-size tomato, chopped

Cook the cauliflower flowerets in boiling salted water with the aniseed or fennel seeds until barely tender (8–10 minutes). Drain and refresh under cold running water. Allow to cool.

Thin down the guacamole with a little water to make a soft, dropping consistency.

Arrange the cauliflower on a serving dish and spread the guacamole on the top. Sprinkle on the chopped tomato and serve.

Ensalada de Nochebuena

BEETROOT, FRUIT AND NUT SALAD

Illustrated on pages 30–31

In Mexico, this traditional Christmas Eve salad would normally include a sprinkling of little, hard multi-coloured sweets [candies], but even my children (who I thought would be bound to love the idea) had reservations about that one. You can prepare the salad in advance and chill it, but leave the peanut and pomegranate garnish till the end or they'll go soggy.

METRIC/IMPERIAL
3 medium beetroots (about 500 g/1 lb),
  cooked, peeled and diced
2 tart green apples (e.g. Granny Smiths),
  cored and diced
2 bananas, peeled and sliced
2 oranges, peeled and chopped
1 lemon, peeled and cut in segments
2 slices fresh pineapple, chopped
lettuce leaves
125 g/4 oz unsalted or dry-roasted peanuts
3 tablespoons pine nuts
seeds from 1 pomegranate
DRESSING:
salt and pepper
150 ml/¼ pint olive oil
4 tablespoons vinegar
1 teaspoon honey

AMERICAN
3 medium-size beets (about 1 lb), cooked,
  peeled and diced
2 tart green apples, cored and diced
2 bananas, peeled and sliced
2 oranges, peeled and chopped
1 lemon, peeled and cut into sections
2 slices fresh pineapple, chopped
lettuce leaves
1 cup raw, unsalted or dry-roasted peanuts
3 tablespoons pine nuts
seeds from 1 pomegranate
DRESSING:
salt and pepper
10 tablespoons olive oil
4 tablespoons vinegar
1 teaspoon honey

In a large bowl, mix together the beetroot, apples, bananas, oranges, lemon and pineapple. Combine the dressing ingredients in a small mixing bowl and blend well. Add to the salad and toss to coat.

    When ready to serve, line a beautiful, round dish with lettuce leaves. Turn out the salad on top and sprinkle on the nuts and pomegranate seeds.

Ensalada de calabacita y ejote

COURGETTE [ZUCCHINI] AND BEAN SALAD

Illustrated on pages 30–31

METRIC/IMPERIAL
350 g/12 oz French beans, trimmed and
  halved
350 g/12 oz courgettes, trimmed and cut in
  lengthwise strips
1 avocado, peeled, stoned and cubed
2 apples or peaches, peeled, cored or
  stoned and chopped
seeds from 1 pomegranate (optional)
DRESSING:
1 egg
120 ml/4 fl oz plain yogurt
salt and pepper
150 ml/¼ pint oil
75 ml/3 fl oz vinegar
1 teaspoon honey
½ clove garlic, peeled and crushed

AMERICAN
¾ lb green beans, trimmed and halved
¾ lb zucchini, trimmed and cut in
  lengthwise strips
1 avocado, peeled, seeded and cubed
2 apples or peaches, peeled, cored or pitted
  and chopped
seeds from 1 pomegranate (optional)
DRESSING:
1 egg
½ cup plain yogurt
salt and pepper
¼ cup oil
6 tablespoons vinegar
1 teaspoon honey
½ clove garlic, peeled and crushed

Cook the beans and courgettes [zucchini] in lightly salted boiling water until just tender. Drain and refresh under cold running water to set the colour.

Place all the dressing ingredients in a blender or food processor and blend well to mix. Pour the dressing over the beans and courgettes [zucchini] and toss to coat.

Mix in the avocado, apples or peaches and pomegranate seeds, if used. Serve well chilled.

CHILES RELLENOS EN FRÍO

MARINATED STUFFED PEPPERS

There are myriad recipes for cold stuffed chillies and peppers, and the detailed instructions here for the preparation and marinating are a model for the variations which follow. Of course, in Mexico the large, dark green *chiles poblanos* would be used. These are full of flavour and sometimes with quite a bite to them. Here we have to make do with green peppers, but provided you use nice big, fresh, firm ones and prepare them as directed, as well as adding a bit of bite to either the marinade or filling, they do very nicely. They make delicious and unusual salad appetizers and can (indeed must) be prepared ahead of time.

METRIC/IMPERIAL

6 large, firm, even-sized green peppers
  (about 150 g/5 oz each)
2 tablespoons olive oil
1 large onion, peeled and thinly sliced
1–2 fresh green chillies, seeded and cut in
  thin strips
250 ml/8 fl oz water
120 ml/4 fl oz white wine vinegar or lemon
  juice
salt and pepper
dried oregano
crushed coriander seeds, or a few sprigs
  fresh coriander

AMERICAN

6 large, firm, equal-sized sweet green
  peppers (about 5 oz each)
2 tablespoons olive oil
1 large onion, peeled and thinly sliced
1–2 fresh green chillies, seeded and cut
  into thin strips
1 cup water
½ cup white wine vinegar or lemon juice
salt and pepper
dried oregano
crushed coriander seeds, or few sprigs
  fresh coriander

At least one day before you plan to serve the peppers, prepare them for the marinade. Using an open gas flame or grill [broiler] heated to maximum, char the peppers on all sides until evenly blistered. The whole process will take about 15–20 minutes. They will crackle and pop and look considerably hot and bothered, but should not become too charred or blackened or you will have trouble peeling them and they will be very soft. Wrap them in a dish towel as they are ready, then place the whole package in a plastic bag and leave them to sweat while you get on with the rest.

Fry the onion, garlic and chilli strips in the oil until soft, then add the water, vinegar or lemon juice, and oregano, coriander, salt and pepper to taste and simmer 10 minutes.

Rub the skins off the peppers under cold running water. Without dislodging the stalk, make a careful slit down one side and pull out the seeds, trying to keep the pepper as intact as possible. Add them to the simmering marinade and let them cook 5 minutes on one side, then turn carefully and give them another 5 minutes on the other side.

Remove the peppers with a slotted spoon. Turn up the heat and let the marinade reduce to about 4–5 tablespoons. Put the prepared peppers on a large plate or dish and pour over the reduced marinade. Leave them in a cool place for at least 6 hours, or better still till the next day, before filling with any of the suggestions on the next two pages.

Chiles rellenos de guacamole

PEPPERS WITH AVOCADO FILLING

METRIC/IMPERIAL
1 clove garlic, peeled
1 teaspoon salt
1–2 fresh green chillies
handful of fresh coriander
2 avocados, peeled and stoned
1 small tomato, chopped
1 tablespoon chopped onion
juice of 1 lime
6 large green peppers, peeled, marinated as
  in master recipe and drained
seeds from 1 pomegranate
fresh coriander or parsley sprigs to
  garnish

AMERICAN
1 clove garlic, peeled
1 teaspoon salt
1–2 fresh green chilies
handful of fresh coriander
2 avocados, peeled and seeded
1 small tomato, chopped
1 tablespoon chopped onion
juice of 1 lime
6 large sweet green peppers, peeled,
  marinated as in master recipe and
  drained
seeds from 1 pomegranate
fresh coriander or parsley sprigs for
  garnish

Mash the garlic, salt, chillies and coriander to a paste in a pestle and mortar (or food processor or blender, if you really have to . . .). Mash in the avocado. Stir in the tomato, onion and lime juice.

    Stuff the drained peppers with the mixture, and garnish with pomegranate seeds and coriander or parsley sprigs.

Chiles rellenos de frijól

PEPPERS WITH BEAN AND SARDINE FILLING

Illustrated on page 52

The mixture of beans and sardines sounds a funny one, but it comes up often in Mexican dishes and is surprisingly successful. Try it – it's a happy combination.

METRIC/IMPERIAL
400 g/14 oz cooked pinto beans (about ½ the
  recipe quantity for *frijoles de olla*, see
  page 140), or 1 400-g/14-oz can pinto beans
pinch of dried oregano
1 *chile chipotle en adobo* (see Glossary –
  optional)
salt
1 tablespoon lard
1 can sardines, drained
6 large green peppers, peeled, marinated as
  in master recipe and drained
125 g/4 oz fresh white cheese, cut into 6
  slices
250 ml/8 fl oz thick sour cream or *crème
  fraiche*
1–2 tomatoes, sliced
wafer-thin onion rings to garnish

AMERICAN
14 oz cooked pinto beans (about ½ the
  recipe quantity for *frijoles de olla*, see
  page 140), or 1 16-oz can pinto beans
pinch of dried oregano
1 *chile chipotle en adobo* (see Glossary –
  optional)
salt
1 tablespoon lard
1 can sardines, drained
6 large sweet green peppers, peeled,
  marinated as in master recipe and
  drained
¼ lb fresh white cheese, cut into 6 slices
1 cup thick sour cream or *crème fraiche*
1–2 tomatoes, sliced
wafer-thin onion rings for garnish

Purée the beans in a blender or food processor with their cooking liquid, or liquid from can, the oregano, chilli and salt to taste, then fry in the hot lard until a fairly dry paste. Add the drained sardines, mashing with the back of a wooden spoon until well incorporated.

Cool a little, then pack into the drained peppers with a slice of cheese each. Arrange on a round dish, stalks outwards. Season the cream with a little salt and pepper and pour over the peppers. Garnish with tomato slices and onion rings.

Chiles rellenos de papa con aguacate

PEPPERS WITH POTATO AND AVOCADO FILLING

METRIC/IMPERIAL
6 large green peppers, peeled and
  marinated as in master recipe
2 avocados, peeled and stoned
125 g/4 oz cream cheese
350 g/12 oz potatoes, peeled, cooked and
  cubed
1 large tomato (about 150 g/5 oz), chopped
salt and pepper
radish 'flowers'
parsley sprigs
SAUCE:
2 courgettes (about 250 g/8 oz), sliced and
  lightly cooked
1 small onion, peeled and chopped
3–4 tablespoons sour cream or *crème fraiche*
salt

AMERICAN
6 large sweet green peppers, peeled and
  marinated as in master recipe
2 avocados, peeled and seeded
¼ lb cream cheese
¾ lb potatoes, peeled, cooked and cubed
1 large tomato (about 5 oz), chopped
salt and pepper
radish 'flowers'
parsley sprigs
SAUCE:
2 zucchini (about ½ lb), sliced and lightly
  cooked
1 small onion, peeled and chopped
3–4 tablespoons sour cream or *crème fraiche*
salt

Drain the peppers, reserving the marinade. Set aside.

Mash one of the avocados with the cream cheese. Mix in the potatoes, tomato and the reserved marinade. Taste for seasoning, adjusting if necessary. Do not overblend the mixture: it should have some texture. Pack into the peppers.

To make the sauce (which should only be done shortly before serving, otherwise the avocado discolours), place the courgettes, second avocado, onion, cream and salt to taste in a food processor or blender and blend until smooth. Spoon over the filled peppers and garnish with radish 'flowers' and parsley sprigs.

Tostadas

CRISPY TORTILLAS WITH VARIOUS TOPPINGS

Illustrated on pages 30–31

Described aptly by Diana Kennedy as a sort of edible plate, these are tortillas dried out to a crisp (or deep-fried), topped with meat, sauce, shredded lettuce, puréed beans, sour cream and all manner of delights. Impossible to eat, as it all either goes up your nose or falls onto your shoes, but deliciously typical of the Mexican love of contrasting textures, flavours and colours.

Tostadas de frijól con pollo

TOSTADAS WITH BEAN AND CHICKEN TOPPING

METRIC/IMPERIAL	AMERICAN
12 thin tortillas, about 15 cm/6 inches in diameter	12 thin tortillas, about 6 inches in diameter
oil	oil
salt	salt
350 g/12 oz puréed pinto or black beans (see pages 140–141)	1½ cups puréed pinto or black beans (see pages 140–141)
1 small lettuce, finely shredded	1 small head lettuce, finely shredded
2–3 tablespoons vinaigrette	2–3 tablespoons vinaigrette
2 tomatoes, chopped	2 tomatoes, chopped
about 250 g/8 oz cooked chicken meat, shredded	about ½ lb cooked chicken meat, shredded (1–1½ cups)
120 ml/4 fl oz sour cream or *crème fraiche*	½ cup sour cream or *crème fraiche*
50 g/2 oz Parmesan cheese, grated	½ cup grated Parmesan cheese

Brush the tortillas with a little oil, sprinkle with salt and dry out in a low oven (100 c/200 f/gas ¼) for about 1 hour until crisp (no longer or they get rather hard). Alternatively you can deep-fry them and drain well on paper towels.

When ready to serve, spread each tortilla with some bean purée, and top with shredded lettuce moistened with vinaigrette, chopped tomatoes, meat, cream and grated cheese. Arrange on a large tray and serve immediately.

Tostadas de guacamole

TOSTADAS WITH AVOCADO TOPPING

METRIC/IMPERIAL	AMERICAN
12 thin tortillas, about 15 cm/6 inches in diameter, prepared as above	12 thin tortillas, about 6 inches in diameter, prepared as above
1 quantity *guacamole* with diced tomato (see page 34)	1 quantity *guacamole* with diced tomato (see page 34)
125 g/4 oz crumbly fresh cheese	¼ lb crumbly fresh cheese
wafer-thin onion rings	wafer-thin onion rings

Spread the prepared tortillas with guacamole, sprinkle on the cheese and garnish with the onion rings. Arrange on a large dish or tray and serve immediately before they go soggy.

Tostadas de papa con sardina

TOSTADAS WITH POTATO AND SARDINE TOPPING

METRIC/IMPERIAL	AMERICAN
1 100-g/4-oz can sardines	1 4-oz can sardines
1 small onion, peeled and finely chopped	1 small onion, peeled and finely chopped
1 fresh green chilli, finely chopped	1 fresh green chili, finely chopped
250 g/8 oz waxy potatoes, cooked, peeled and cubed	½ lb waxy potatoes, cooked, peeled and cubed
1 large tomato (about 150 g/5 oz), peeled and chopped	1 large tomato (about 5 oz), peeled and chopped
salt and pepper	salt and pepper
12 thin tortillas, about 15 cm/6 inches in diameter, prepared as above	12 thin tortillas, about 6 inches in diameter, prepared as above
sour cream or *crème fraiche*	sour cream or *crème fraiche*
chopped parsley	chopped parsley

Using some of the oil from the sardine can, fry the onion and chilli very gently until golden. Add the potato cubes, tomato and mashed sardine and continue to fry, stirring and turning, until well mixed and crusty. Season to taste with salt and pepper and spread on the prepared tortillas. Add a dollop of sour cream and some chopped parsley. Arrange on a large dish or tray and serve immediately before they go soggy.

Tostadas de papa con chorizo

TOSTADAS WITH POTATO AND SAUSAGE TOPPING

METRIC/IMPERIAL	AMERICAN
2 chorizos or pure pork sausages (about 250 g/8 oz), skinned and crumbled	12 thin tortillas, about 6 inches in diameter, prepared as above
1 small onion, peeled and finely chopped	2 chorizos or pork link sausages (about ½ lb), skinned and crumbled
1 fresh green or red chilli, finely chopped	1 small onion, peeled and finely chopped
250 g/8 oz waxy potatoes, cooked, peeled and cubed	1 fresh green or red chili, finely chopped
salt and pepper	½ lb waxy potatoes, cooked, peeled and cubed
12 thin tortillas, about 15 cm/6 inches in diameter, prepared as above	salt and pepper
1 large tomato (about 150 g/5 oz), peeled and chopped	1 large tomato (about 5 oz), peeled and chopped
sour cream or *crème fraiche*	sour cream or *crème fraiche*
parsley sprigs	parsley sprigs

Fry the crumbled chorizos or sausages without any extra fat until their own fat is rendered. Add the onion, chilli and potatoes and continue to fry, stirring, for about 5 minutes to combine the flavours. Season to taste with salt and pepper. Sprinkle on to the prepared tortillas, garnish with the tomato dice, sour cream or *crème fraiche* and decorate with the parsley sprigs. Serve immediately before they go soggy.

CHILES RELLENOS CALIENTES

HOT STUFFED PEPPERS WITH VARIOUS FILLINGS

In addition to the many stuffed green pepper dishes marinated and served cold (see recipes for *chiles rellenos en frío*), there are many possibilities for stuffed peppers to be served hot. In Mexico, like many of the dishes which I have indicated as suitable for first courses, they would usually be served as a vegetable course either with or just after the main dish. However, as some of them are a bit elaborate, I think they do better standing on their own as appetizers.

Chiles rellenos de mariscos

PEPPERS STUFFED WITH SHELLFISH
IN CREAM OR CHEESE SAUCE

METRIC/IMPERIAL	AMERICAN
6 large, even-sized green peppers (about 150 g/5 oz each)	6 large, equal-sized sweet green peppers (about 5 oz each)
1 small onion, peeled and finely chopped	1 small onion, peeled and finely chopped
1 small fresh green chilli, seeded and finely chopped	1 small fresh green chili, seeded and finely chopped
25 g/1 oz butter, or 1 tablespoon oil	2 tablespoons butter, or 1 tablespoon oil
1 large tomato (about 150 g/5 oz), peeled, seeded and chopped	1 large tomato (about 5 oz), peeled, seeded and chopped
about 350 g/12 oz mixed prepared shellfish, preferably raw	about ¾ lb mixed prepared shellfish, preferably raw
pinch of dried oregano	pinch of dried oregano
250 ml/8 fl oz double cream, *crème fraiche*, or light cheese sauce	1 cup thick cream, *crème fraiche* or light cheese sauce

Prepare the peppers as in *chiles rellenos de queso* (page 54). Preheat the oven to moderate (180 c, 350 f, gas 4).

Soften the onion and chilli in the butter or oil without browning. Add the tomato, raise the heat and fry till the liquid is evaporated and the mixture is thick and syrupy. Stir in the prepared shellfish and oregano and continue frying until just cooked through – don't overcook or you'll toughen the shellfish. Cool a little, then fill the prepared peppers with the mixture.

Place the peppers in a lightly greased baking dish. Season the cream with a little salt and pepper and pour over the peppers (or coat with the cheese sauce). Bake for 20–30 minutes until golden and well heated through.

Right *guacamole* (page 34)
Overleaf *tortillas de maíz* (page 17) on the left and *tortillas de harina* (page 18) on the right, with a selection of fillings for *tacos* and *burritos*: chicken (page 75); creamy chilli, pepper and onion (page 74); minced meat, nuts and fruit (page 75); scrambled egg and sausage (page 81)

Chiles rellenos de elote

PEPPERS STUFFED WITH CORN IN TOMATO SAUCE

METRIC/IMPERIAL	AMERICAN
6 large, even-sized green peppers (about 150 g/5 oz each)	6 large, equal-sized sweet green peppers (about 5 oz each)
1 medium onion, peeled and finely chopped	1 medium-size onion, peeled and finely chopped
2 cloves garlic, peeled and chopped	2 cloves garlic, peeled and chopped
1 tablespoon lard or oil	1 tablespoon lard or oil
kernels from 2 corn cobs, or 350 g/12 oz frozen corn kernels	kernels from 2 ears of corn, or $\frac{3}{4}$ lb (about $2\frac{1}{4}$ cups) frozen whole kernel corn
1–2 fresh green chillies, seeded and finely chopped	1–2 fresh green chilies, seeded and finely chopped
finely chopped fresh *epazote* (optional)	finely chopped fresh *epazote* (optional)
salt	salt
75 g/3 oz cream cheese	3 oz cream cheese
1 quantity *caldillo de jitomate* (see page 36)	1 quantity *caldillo de jitomate* (see page 36)

Prepare the peppers as in *chiles rellenos de queso* (page 54). Preheat the oven to moderate (180 c, 350 f, gas 4).

Soften the onion and garlic in the lard or oil without browning, then add the corn kernels, chillies and *epazote*, if used. Cover and cook for about 10 minutes or until the corn is just tender, stirring from time to time to prevent sticking. Season with salt – it can stand quite a lot, as the corn seems to absorb a great deal. Mix in the cream cheese to bind it all together and cool a little.

Fill the prepared peppers with the corn mixture and place them in a lightly greased baking dish. (Can be prepared ahead of time up to this point.) Pour over the tomato sauce and bake for 20 minutes or until well heated through and the sauce is bubbling hot.

Left *chiles rellenos de frijól* (page 44)

Chiles rellenos de queso

PEPPERS STUFFED WITH CHEESE IN TOMATO SAUCE

This dish is a good example of the exciting blend of colours and textures which is so much a feature of Mexican food: green peppers with a slight crunch to them, white melting cheese in the middle, sharp red tomato sauce with quite a bite to it. I have to admit that they're a bit of a bother to make, but all the donkey work can be done in advance, leaving only the final frying and saucing. The tomato sauce (see recipe for *caldillo de jitomate*, page 36, for detailed instructions) can be frozen, as can the peeled peppers. 'Why peel peppers, when they're so good with their skins on?', you may be asking, as Julia Child did in her book *Julia Child & More Company** and goes on to answer the question more than adequately with illustrations and text, claiming that the resulting beast has 'a flavour completely different from what you taste in, say, a baked stuffed pepper . . . very subtle and tender with an exquisite flavour, *and* the colour remains very bright.' So you see, it's not just me, being perverse and perfectionist . . .

METRIC/IMPERIAL	AMERICAN
6 large, even-sized green peppers (about 150 g/5 oz each)	6 large, equal-sized sweet green peppers (about 5 oz each)
1 quantity *caldillo de jitomate* (see page 36)	1 quantity *caldillo de jitomate* (see page 36)
6 fat slices mature Cheddar cheese, cut the same length and width as the peppers	6 fat sl ces sharp Cheddar cheese, cut the same length and width as the peppers
4–5 tablespoons cooking oil	4–5 tablespoons cooking oil
3 eggs, separated	3 eggs, separated
salt and pepper	salt and pepper
flour	flour

Working either directly on a gas flame, or using a grill [broiler] at maximum heat, sear the peppers all over, turning with tongs or protected fingers until the skin is a mass of beautiful blisters. Remove the peppers as they are charred, wrap them in a dish towel and put the whole package inside a plastic bag to sweat for up to 20 minutes (no longer, or the peppers will get too soft and fall apart when you come to fry them).

Meanwhile, prepare the tomato sauce in a pan which will be big enough to hold the 6 peppers later on.

Rub the skins off the peppers under running water. Leaving the stalks intact, make a careful incision down one side. Pull out the seeds very gently, and resist the temptation to pull out any of the veins attached or the whole thing will fall apart. The stalks will be a valuable handle later on when you come to the frying stage. Fill each pepper with a slice of cheese and close it up with a wooden toothpick, overlapping the seams a bit so the cheese doesn't ooze out later. Leave to dry on paper towels. (Can be prepared up to this point, and even frozen in this state.)

When ready to fry the peppers, heat the oil in a large sauté or frying pan (the oil should be to a depth of about 1 cm/½ inch). Quickly beat the egg whites into stiff peaks with a pinch of salt, then briefly beat in the egg yolks. Dust the

Julia Child & More Company, pub. Alfred Knopf.

filled peppers with seasoned flour and, holding each one by its stalk, dip and twirl it about in the egg mixture to coat evenly. Place immediately in the hot oil and fry on all sides until evenly golden. Remove the peppers as they are ready and drain on paper towels.

Just before serving, place the peppers in the hot tomato sauce, which has been conveniently simmering just nearby, and bring them to the table. (Alternatively, you could keep them hot in a gratin dish for a little while in a low oven and pour over the sauce at the last minute: don't let them linger too long in the sauce though, or they'll lose the lovely crispness of the feather-light batter.)

QUESADILLAS

TORTILLA TURNOVERS

Reminiscent of pasties or *empanadas*, these are freshly pressed out, raw tortillas filled with a variety of fillings, folded over and pinched together. Do a selection for a party, making them up ahead of time. Then either leave them on a baking sheet covered with a damp dish towel, or open-freeze them on a tray or cake rack for easy removal from the freezer as needed. To serve, either brush with oil and bake in a preheated moderately hot oven (200 C, 400 F, gas 6), or deep fry until golden brown and crispy. All *quesadillas* can be served with any of the sauces in the table sauce section, but *salsa mexicana* (see page 34) goes particularly well.

Masa para quesadillas

QUESADILLA DOUGH

METRIC/IMPERIAL
300 g/10 oz *tortilla* flour
4 tablespoons plain white flour
1 teaspoon baking powder
½ teaspoon salt
about 300 ml/½ pint hand-hot water
120 ml/4 fl oz double cream, or 65 g/2½ oz
 cream cheese
1½ tablespoons lard

AMERICAN
2¼ cups *tortilla* flour
¼ cup all-purpose flour
1 teaspoon baking powder
½ teaspoon salt
about 1¼ cups hand-hot water
½ cup thick cream, or 2½ oz cream cheese
1½ tablespoons lard

Make up the quesadilla dough by mixing together all the ingredients in the order listed and kneading well. Alternatively, blend the ingredients together in a food processor using the metal or plastic blade. The dough should be quite firm but pliable, and should not stick to your hands.

Let the dough rest for a bit while you prepare a selection of fillings, then press or roll out to 15 cm/6 inch rounds, following the detailed instructions for making tortillas on page 17, and fill with any of the following. Each filling is enough for 10 *quesadillas*. After filling, fold the rounds over in half and press the edges well to seal. Bake or fry as instructed above. *Makes about 24.*

Quesadillas de hongo

MUSHROOM OR HUITLACOCHE FILLING

METRIC/IMPERIAL	AMERICAN
½ onion, peeled and finely chopped	½ onion, peeled and finely chopped
1 clove garlic, peeled and crushed	1 clove garlic, peeled and minced
1–2 fresh chillies, finely chopped	1–2 fresh green chilies, finely chopped
25 g/1 oz butter or lard	2 tablespoons butter or lard
350 g/12 oz mushrooms or *huitlacoche* (see Glossary), finely chopped	¾ lb mushrooms or *huitlacoche*, finely chopped
salt and pepper	salt and pepper
2–3 tablespoons double cream or *crème fraiche*	2–3 tablespoons thick cream or *crème fraiche*
chopped fresh *epazote* (optional)	chopped fresh *epazote* (optional)

Soften the onion, garlic and chillies in the butter or lard without browning. Add the mushrooms or *huitlacoche*, and season to taste with salt and pepper. Cover and cook for about 10 minutes or until the juices run.

Remove the cover, raise the heat and cook until the juices have almost evaporated. Stir in the cream and *epazote*, if used. Cool a little before filling the pressed-out dough rounds. Bake or fry as directed on page 55.

Quesadillas de flor

COURGETTE [ZUCCHINI] FLOWER FILLING

METRIC/IMPERIAL	AMERICAN
20 courgette flowers	20 zucchini flowers
1 shallot or ½ onion, peeled and chopped	1 shallot or ½ onion, peeled and chopped
25 g/1 oz butter	2 tablespoons butter
1 teaspoon oil	1 teaspoon oil
chopped fresh *epazote* (optional)	chopped fresh *epazote* (optional)
salt and pepper	salt and pepper
3–4 tablespoons double cream or *crème fraiche*	3–4 tablespoons heavy cream or *crème fraiche*

Pull off the spiky bits from around the outside of the flower base and separate the flowers from the stalks. Chop the flowers roughly and set aside. Strip the stalks as if peeling celery and chop roughly. Soften the stalks with the shallot or onion in the butter and oil without browning. Add the roughly chopped flowers, *epazote*, if used, and salt and pepper to taste. Cover and cook for about 10 minutes.

Raise the heat, uncover and fry till fairly dry. Stir in the cream. Cool a little before filling the pressed-out dough rounds. Bake or fry as directed on page 55.

Quesadillas de queso

CHEESE FILLING

METRIC/IMPERIAL
250 g/8 oz Cheddar or raclette cheese
fresh *epazote* leaves (optional)
salt
2–3 fresh green chillies, seeded and cut in
  very fine strips

AMERICAN
½ lb Cheddar or raclette cheese
fresh *epazote* leaves (optional)
salt
2–3 fresh green chilies, seeded and cut
  into fine strips

Cut the cheese in slices the same length as the tortillas and half the width. Place on one side of each pressed-out dough round and add an *epazote* leaf if you should be so lucky as to have one, plus a pinch of salt and a strip or two of chilli. Fold over, seal the edges well And bake or fry as directed on page 55. This is the absolute best (and simplest) of all the fillings, and super for a quick supper, especially if you have pre-frozen the *quesadillas* as indicated.

Quesadillas de frijól

BEAN AND TOMATO FILLING

METRIC/IMPERIAL
½ onion, peeled and finely chopped
1 clove garlic, peeled and crushed
1 tablespoon lard
1 large tomato (about 150 g/5 oz), peeled
  and chopped
1 400-g/14-oz can pinto beans, puréed with
  some of their liquid, or ½ quantity *frijoles
  de olla* (see page 140)

AMERICAN
½ onion, peeled and finely chopped
1 clove garlic, peeled and minced
1 tablespoon lard
1 large tomato (about 5 oz), peeled and
  chopped
1 16-oz can pinto beans, puréed with
  some of their liquid, or ½ quantity *frijoles
  de olla* (see page 140)

Brown the onion and garlic in the lard. Add the tomato and fry, stirring, until the mixture dries out a bit. Add the bean purée and continue frying for quite a while till in a fairly thick paste – it plops about rather alarmingly, so use a fairly deep, heavy pan. Cool a little before filling the pressed-out dough rounds.

Quesadillas de papa con chorizo

POTATO AND SAUSAGE FILLING

METRIC/IMPERIAL
250 g/8 oz chorizos or pure pork sausages,
  skinned and crumbled
250 g/8 oz waxy potatoes, cooked, peeled
  and cubed
1–2 *chiles chipotles en adobo*, seeded
  (optional)
salt and pepper

AMERICAN
½ lb chorizos or pure pork link sausages,
  skinned and crumbled
½ lb waxy potatoes, cooked, peeled and
  cubed
1–2 *chiles chipotles en adobo*, seeded
  (optional)
salt and pepper

Fry the sausages until the fat runs (adding a little extra lard only if necessary: some sausages are extremely fatty already). Add the potato cubes, chillies, if used, (you must seed them – they're absolute fire) and salt and pepper to taste. Continue to fry, stirring, until well mixed and tasty. Cool a little before filling the pressed-out dough rounds. Bake or fry as directed.

Crepas con salsa de nuez

CHICKEN CRÊPES WITH CREAMY *CHIPOTLE* AND WALNUT SAUCE

For those lucky enough to be able to find these little, smoked chillies in cans, here is a lovely, quick, simple and tasty recipe.

METRIC/IMPERIAL
12 crêpes (see recipe for *crepas de flor*,
  page 59)
2 chicken breasts or legs, cooked, boned
  and shredded
120 ml/4 fl oz thick sour cream or *crème
  fraiche*
125 g/4 oz shelled walnuts
250 ml/8 fl oz double cream or *crème fraiche*
2 *chiles chipotles en adobo*, seeded
salt
little chicken stock

AMERICAN
12 crêpes (see recipe for *crepas de flor*,
  page 59)
2 chicken breast halves or legs, cooked,
  boned and shredded
½ cup thick sour cream or *crème fraiche*
1 cup shelled walnuts
1 cup heavy cream or *crème fraiche*
2 *chiles chipotles en adobo*, seeded
salt
little chicken stock

Preheat the oven to moderate (180 c, 350 f, gas 4).

Fill the prepared crêpes with the shredded chicken and sour cream, and roll up. Place side by side in a lightly buttered baking dish. Blend together the walnuts, double [heavy] cream, chillies and salt in a food processor or blender, adding only enough stock to make a light coating consistency. Pour over the crêpes.

Bake for 20–25 minutes, or until well heated through and bubbly.

Crepas de flor

CRÊPES STUFFED WITH COURGETTE [ZUCCHINI] FLOWERS

METRIC/IMPERIAL	AMERICAN
about 50 courgette flowers	about 50 zucchini flowers
1 shallot or ½ onion, peeled and finely chopped	1 shallot or ½ onion, peeled and finely chopped
1 clove garlic, peeled and crushed	1 clove garlic, peeled and minced
25 g/1 oz butter	2 tablespoons butter
1 teaspoon oil	1 teaspoon oil
finely chopped fresh *epazote* leaves (optional)	finely chopped fresh *epazote* leaves (optional)
salt and pepper	salt and pepper
3–4 tablespoons double cream or *crème fraiche*	3–4 tablespoons thick cream or *crème fraiche*
2–3 tablespoons freshly grated Parmesan cheese	2–3 tablespoons freshly grated Parmesan cheese
CRÊPE BATTER:	CRÊPE BATTER:
225 ml/7½ fl oz milk	scant cup milk
225 ml/7½ fl oz water	scant cup water
4 eggs	4 eggs
1 teaspoon salt	1 teaspoon salt
225 g/8 oz plain flour	2 cups all-purpose flour
4 tablespoons salad oil	¼ cup salad oil

Blend together the ingredients for the crêpe batter and leave to rest while you prepare the filling.

Separate the courgette [zucchini] flowers from the stalks, and discard the spiky bits around the base of the flower. Chop the flowers roughly. Strip the stalks as if you were peeling celery and chop them. Soften the stalks with the shallot or onion and garlic in the butter and oil without browning. Add the chopped flowers, *epazote*, if using, and salt and pepper to taste. Cover and cook for 5–10 minutes or until the juices run, then uncover, raise the heat and fry rapidly until the juice evaporates. Stir in the cream – just enough to bind the mixture a bit – and set aside to cool.

Preheat the oven to moderate (180 c, 350 F, gas 4).

Make 12 of the thinnest, laciest crêpes you can achieve (there'll be more batter than you need for this recipe, but while you're at it you might as well freeze some). Fill with the mixture, roll up and place side by side in a lightly buttered baking dish. (You can prepare the whole dish up to this point and then refrigerate. I don't advise freezing, as most of the courgette [zucchini] flower dishes lose their delicate flavour in the freezer.) Sprinkle the crêpes with the Parmesan and bake 10–15 minutes or until well heated through but not too crisp.

BRUNCHES, LUNCHES, SUPPERS AND INFORMAL PARTIES

Into this category come a whole host of tortilla dishes, some eggs, and a few odds and ends to round off the chapter. Don't forget, too, that Mexican food lends itself to big parties: families are enormous, even nowadays, and then there are all those beaming maids and wrinkled retainers to feed too, not to mention the two or three friends who 'just happened to drop in as we were leaving'. Many of these dishes, therefore, are highly expandable to allow for a rather loosely defined number of eaters, and do as well for an informal party as for a family supper. Since many of them are tortilla-based, the recipes for both corn and wheat tortillas are repeated in this chapter for easy reference.

Tortillas de maíz	Corn tortillas
Enchiladas	Gratinéed tortilla dishes
de mole	with chilli and nut sauce
norteñas	with pork filling in creamy chilli sauce
revueltas	with chicken filling in tomato sauce
con acelgas	with chard filling
vegetarianas	in tomato sauce with vegetables and cheese
de pollo	with creamy chicken, green pepper and chilli filling
Chilaquiles	Tortilla casseroles
bravos	with red chilli and tomato sauce
iniciados	with creamy green sauce
rojos	with spicy tomato sauce
Tacos	Filled corn tortillas
de rajas	creamy chilli, pepper and onion
de picadillo	minced meat, nuts and fruits
de pollo	chicken
Pastel delicia	'Emergency rations' tortilla pie
Budin azteca	Fancy tortilla pie
Tortillas de harina	Wheat tortillas
Burritos	Filled wheat tortillas
queso fundido	cheese
mochomos	shredded beef
frijól y queso	bean and cheese
huevos revueltos con chorizo	scrambled egg and sausage
Sincronizadas	Tortilla ham and cheese sandwich
Huevos	Eggs
rancheros	fried with beans and tomato sauce
en rabo de mestiza	poached in tomato sauce
revueltos a la mexicana	scrambled with spicy tomato sauce
Molletes	Toasted buns with beans and cheese
Pastes pachuqueños	Mexican Cornish pasties from Pachuca
Tamal de cazuela	Baked chicken and pork cornmeal pie

Tortillas de maíz

CORN TORTILLAS

Illustrated on page 12 and pages 50–51

METRIC/IMPERIAL	AMERICAN
250 g/8 oz *tortilla* flour	2 cups *tortilla* flour
50 g/2 oz plain white flour	½ cup all-purpose flour
about 350 ml/12 fl oz hand-hot water	about 1½ cups hand-hot water

Mix together (or process using the plastic blade of a food processor) the two flours and the water (don't add any salt). Let the dough rest, covered with a damp cloth, for about 30 minutes. Meanwhile, cut two 15 cm/6 inch discs from a plastic bag.

Heat a large griddle or heavy frying pan. Take a piece of dough about the size of a golf ball and roll it out thinly and evenly with a rolling pin between the two discs of plastic, rotating at each roll to get a roughly even circle of about 15 cm/6 inches in diameter, and 2 mm/$\frac{1}{16}$ inch thick. Alternatively, use a tortilla press. Peel off the top layer of plastic and transfer the tortilla from the bottom plastic on to your hand, letting about half the tortilla hang over the outer edge of your hand. Then lay (rather than hurl) the tortilla down on the hot griddle or pan. You should hear a slightly protesting sizzle, and in about 60 seconds the tortilla will have puffed up and be done on one side. (If you leave it any longer it will get hard, and if it's not done in the time, turn up the heat a bit. As with crêpes, the first few are always best fed to the dog.) Turn it over and cook the second side.

Put the tortilla on a cloth-lined plate or basket, cover it up and keep warm as you continue in the same way with the rest of the dough. Tortillas will keep for 4–5 days in their cloth, overwrapped in a plastic bag, in the refrigerator, and they freeze perfectly. *Makes about 24.*

ENCHILADAS

Enchiladas, in case you haven't met them before, are tortillas dunked in a sauce, filled or topped with something delicious and then heated through in the oven (or served right away, if you've worked fast). They are enormously versatile and a very useful supper dish for using up leftovers, or expanded to make the perfect buffet party dish. Mexican recipes invariably direct that you pre-fry the tortillas before dipping in the sauce, filling and rolling up, but this seems to me an unnecessary step: they can be made pliable on a griddle without the addition of extra fat and more frying pans.

The tortillas should be slightly stale: in other words leathery, but definitely not crisp. If they are too fresh they will absorb too much sauce and disintegrate; if crisp they will not absorb sufficient sauce and will be tough.

Enchiladas de mole

ENCHILADAS WITH CHILLI AND NUT SAUCE

These are delicious on their own for supper, or as a savoury accompaniment to the famous *carne asada a la tampiqueña* (see page 114). In Mexico you'd probably buy your *mole* in a paste ready-prepared from the market, or if you've fearlessly done the recipe for *mole poblano* on page 124, you'll have your own home-grown version. If not, here is a simpler one:

METRIC/IMPERIAL	AMERICAN
3 *chiles anchos*, or 3 tablespoons chilli powder	3 *chiles anchos*, or 3 tablespoons chili powder
3 large tomatoes (about 500 g/1 lb)	3 large tomatoes (about 1 lb)
1 cm/½ inch piece of cinnamon stick	½ inch piece of cinnamon stick
2–3 cloves	2–3 cloves
1 clove garlic	1 clove garlic
25 g/1 oz unsalted peanuts	¼ cup raw unsalted peanuts
25 g/1 oz blanched almonds	¼ cup blanched almonds
1 slice white or French bread, cubed	1 slice white or French bread, cubed
2 tablespoons lard or oil	2 tablespoons lard or oil
pinch of dried oregano	pinch of dried oregano
pinch of sugar	pinch of sugar
salt	salt
stock or water	stock or water
18 stale tortillas	18 stale tortillas
250 g/8 oz crumbly white cheese	½ lb crumbly white cheese
finely chopped onion	finely chopped onion
2 tablespoons sesame seeds	2 tablespoons sesame seeds

Toast the whole chillies, tomatoes, cinnamon, cloves and garlic in a heavy frying pan or griddle. Remove stalks and seeds from the chillies, tear in bits and soak in hot water for 20 minutes. Peel the garlic. Quarter the tomatoes.

Fry the peanuts, almonds and bread cubes in 1 tablespoon lard. Scrape into a food processor or blender and add the drained chilli pieces (or chilli powder), garlic, tomatoes, spices, oregano, sugar, and salt to taste. Blend until smooth. Sieve or push through a food mill.

Heat the remaining lard or oil in the almond/peanut frying pan, and fry the sauce till thick and syrupy. Dilute to a coating consistency with stock or water.

Heat through the tortillas until supple on a griddle or in a heavy ungreased frying pan, then dip into the sauce and roll up or fold over. Arrange in a heated serving dish. Sprinkle on the cheese, chopped onion and sesame seeds. Serve immediately.

Enchiladas norteñas

ENCHILADAS WITH PORK FILLING IN CREAMY CHILLI SAUCE

In this recipe, unlike in others where dried chillies are called for, you can't substitute chilli powder as you need the body of the whole chillies to give the sauce bulk. It's worth hunting them down, for this and other recipes.

METRIC/IMPERIAL	AMERICAN
4 *chiles anchos*	4 *chiles anchos*
1 clove garlic	1 clove garlic
500 ml/16 fl oz warm milk	2 cups warm milk
2 teaspoons salt	2 teaspoons salt
1 tablespoon oil or lard	1 tablespoon oil or lard
stock or water	stock or water
18 stale tortillas	18 stale tortillas
400–500 g/14–16 oz cooked pork, shredded	about 1 lb cooked pork, shredded (2 cups)
120 ml/4 fl oz sour cream or *crème fraiche* mixed with 1 teaspoon cornflour and 2 tablespoons milk	$\frac{1}{2}$ cup thick sour cream or *crème fraiche* mixed with 1 teaspoon cornstarch and 2 tablespoons milk
50 g/2 oz Cheddar cheese, grated	$\frac{1}{2}$ cup grated Cheddar cheese
radishes	radishes
shredded lettuce	shredded lettuce
onion rings	onion rings

Toast the whole chillies gently on a griddle or heavy, ungreased frying pan until supple and fragrant. Using scissors or a knife, slit them open, remove stalks and seeds and tear into rough pieces. Soak in hot water for about 20 minutes.

Preheat the oven to moderate (180 C, 350 F, gas 4).

Toast the garlic until soft, then peel it. Blend the garlic with the drained chilli pieces, warm milk and salt in a food processor or blender until quite smooth. Strain this sauce. Heat the oil or lard in a heavy saucepan until nearly smoking, then throw in the strained sauce. Place a splatter shield over the top and cook fairly hard for about 10 minutes or until thick and syrupy. Add enough stock or water to give a lightly coating consistency.

Warm the tortillas on a griddle just enough to make them pliable. Dunk them in the hot sauce one by one, leaving them just long enough to be able to bend them in two without breaking. Fill each one with some pork, fold over and arrange in a long serving dish, overlapping, in a long line.

Spread over any remaining sauce, then cover with the cream mixture. Finally sprinkle with the grated cheese. Bake for about 30 minutes or until well heated through and bubbly. Garnish with radishes, shredded lettuce and wafer-thin onion rings.

Enchiladas revueltas

ENCHILADAS WITH CHICKEN FILLING IN TOMATO SAUCE

METRIC/IMPERIAL	AMERICAN
1 tablespoon sultanas	1 tablespoon raisins
1 tablespoon chopped stoned olives	1 tablespoon chopped pitted olives
1 tablespoon chopped unblanched almonds	1 tablespoon chopped unblanched almonds
250 g/8 oz cooked chicken meat, shredded	$\frac{1}{2}$ lb cooked chicken meat, shredded (1–1$\frac{1}{2}$ cups)
salt	salt
18 stale tortillas	18 stale tortillas
2–3 eggs, lightly beaten	2–3 eggs, lightly beaten
1 quantity *caldillo de jitomate* (see page 36)	1 quantity *caldillo de jitomate* (see page 36)
finely chopped onion	finely chopped onion
radish 'flowers'	radish 'flowers'
shredded lettuce	shredded lettuce

Preheat the oven to moderate (180 c, 350 f, gas 4). Mix together the sultanas, olives, almonds and chicken, salting well. Soften the tortillas on the griddle or in a heavy ungreased frying pan. Dip into the beaten eggs, fill with the chicken mixture and roll up. Arrange in an ovenproof serving dish.

Pour over the tomato sauce and bake for 25–30 minutes or until well heated through and the egg is set. Garnish with onion, radishes and lettuce.

Enchiladas con acelgas

ENCHILADAS IN TOMATO SAUCE WITH CHARD FILLING

METRIC/IMPERIAL	AMERICAN
2 large tomatoes (about 350 g/12 oz)	2 large tomatoes (about $\frac{3}{4}$ lb)
1–2 fresh green chillies	1–2 fresh green chilies
1 clove garlic	1 clove garlic
1 onion, peeled	1 onion, peeled
1 tablespoon lard or oil	1 tablespoon lard or oil
1 litre/1$\frac{3}{4}$ pints stock (or cooking water from chard or spinach)	1 quart stock (or cooking water from chard or spinach)
500 g/1 lb chard or spinach	1 lb chard or spinach
120 ml/4 fl oz + 4–5 tablespoons double cream or *crème fraiche*	$\frac{1}{2}$ cup + 4–5 tablespoons thick cream or *crème fraiche*
salt and pepper	salt and pepper
18 stale tortillas	18 stale tortillas
lard or oil to a depth of 5 mm/$\frac{1}{4}$ inch	lard or oil to a depth of $\frac{1}{4}$ inch
75 g/3 oz Cheddar cheese, grated	$\frac{3}{4}$ cup grated Cheddar cheese
1 tablespoon very finely chopped onion	1 tablespoon very finely chopped onion

Grill [broil] the tomatoes, chillies, garlic and onion. Peel the garlic, then blend these ingredients in a food processor or blender till smooth. Fry in the lard or oil in a big frying pan until well reduced and thick. Add enough stock (or cooking water) to make a lightly coating consistency. Set aside.

Blanch the chard or spinach in boiling water for 5 minutes. Drain, refresh in cold water and squeeze well to dry. Chop roughly, return to the pan and toss over high heat until all juice is evaporated. Add 2–3 tablespoons of the cream, plenty of salt and pepper and mix well.

Preheat the oven to moderate (180 c, 350 f, gas 4).

Fry the tortillas briefly in lard or oil (you want to wilt them only) or heat through on a griddle or heavy ungreased frying pan. Remove with tongs and dunk in the tomato sauce, turning and coating well. Fill with the creamed chard or spinach, roll up and arrange in a buttered gratin dish, in one layer. Pour over any remaining sauce. (The dish can be prepared up to this point, covered with foil and refrigerated or frozen.)

Pour on the remaining cream, sprinkle with the grated cheese and bake for 30–40 minutes or until well heated through and the cheese has melted. (The time they take will depend upon whether they are at room temperature or cold.) Garnish with the onion and serve with a sharply-dressed green salad.

Enchiladas vegetarianas

ENCHILADAS IN TOMATO SAUCE WITH VEGETABLES AND CHEESE

METRIC/IMPERIAL
4 *chiles anchos*, or 4 tablespoons chilli
  powder
2 large tomatoes (about 350 g/12 oz)
1 onion, peeled
1 clove garlic
salt and pepper
1 tablespoon oil or lard
about 250 ml/8 fl oz stock or water
18 stale tortillas
2 carrots, peeled, cooked and diced
2 courgettes, cooked and diced
4 potatoes, cooked, peeled and diced
125 g/4 oz French beans, cut in short
  lengths and lightly cooked
125 g/4 oz Parmesan cheese, grated

AMERICAN
4 *chiles anchos*, or $\frac{1}{4}$ cup chili powder
2 large tomatoes (about $\frac{3}{4}$ lb)
1 onion, peeled
1 clove garlic
salt and pepper
1 tablespoon oil or lard
about 1 cup stock or water
18 stale tortillas
2 carrots, peeled, cooked and diced
2 zucchini, cooked and diced
4 potatoes, cooked, peeled and diced
$\frac{1}{4}$ lb green beans, cut into short lengths
  and lightly cooked
1 cup grated Parmesan cheese

If using whole *chiles anchos*, toast them briefly on a griddle or ungreased heavy frying pan until fragrant and pliable. Turn once or twice and press down with a spatula. Remove, cut open and discard seeds and stalks. Soak in hot water for about 20 minutes.

Toast the tomatoes, onion and garlic on the same griddle. Quarter the tomato and onion and peel the garlic. Place all three in the container of a food processor or blender (with chilli powder if you are using it, or the soaked and drained chilli pieces), add salt and pepper and blend till smooth. Using a large, heavy, deep frying pan, heat the lard or oil till almost smoking, then fry the puréed mixture until well-seasoned and thick. Add just enough stock or water to give a light coating consistency.

Preheat the oven to moderate (180 c, 350 f, gas 4).

When ready to assemble, soften the tortillas on a griddle or heavy frying pan (just enough to make them pliable and receptive to the sauce). Using a pair of tongs, dunk them in the chilli sauce, turning once. Place on an oven-proof serving dish, fold over in four like a hanky and push up to the end of the dish. Continue in this way until all are finished. Sprinkle the cooked vegetables mixed with half of the Parmesan on top, pour over any remaining chilli sauce and sprinkle on the remaining Parmesan. Bake for 20–30 minutes.

Enchiladas de pollo

CHICKEN ENCHILADAS IN CREAMY GREEN PEPPER AND CHILLI
SAUCE

METRIC/IMPERIAL	AMERICAN
1 chicken (about 1.5 kg/3 lb)	1 chicken (about 3 lb)
1 carrot, peeled	1 carrot, peeled
2 onions, peeled	2 onions, peeled
salt and pepper	salt and pepper
herbs to taste	herbs to taste
4 green peppers	4 sweet green peppers
2–3 fresh green chillies	2–3 fresh green chilies
1 clove garlic	1 clove garlic
250 ml/8 fl oz milk (fresh or evaporated)	1 cup milk (fresh or evaporated)
lard or oil	lard or oil
18 stale tortillas	18 stale tortillas
250 ml/8 fl oz double cream or *crème fraiche*	1 cup thick cream or *crème fraiche*
50 g/2 oz Cheddar cheese, grated	½ cup grated Cheddar cheese
shredded lettuce	shredded lettuce
radish 'flowers'	radish 'flowers'

Poach the chicken in water just to cover with the carrot, one of the onions, salt, pepper and herbs until just tender. Cool a little, drain, reserving the stock. Remove the meat from the carcass and shred (pull apart with your fingers). You should have about 500 g/1 lb [2–2½ cups] chicken meat. Return the bones to the stock in the pan and continue simmering to further enrich the chicken stock. Strain and set aside.

Heat the grill [broiler] to maximum (or use an open gas flame) and toast the peppers and chillies, turning until evenly blistered. Peel the peppers by rubbing off the skin under running water, and discard stalks and seeds. Don't try to peel the chillies if they're too small and fiddly – but do remove the stalks and seeds. Blend the peppers and chillies with the second onion, the garlic, milk, and salt to taste in a food processor or blender to a smooth purée. Heat 1 tablespoon lard or oil in a heavy frying pan until almost smoking, pour in the purée and fry, stirring all around, until well-seasoned and thick. Dilute with only enough chicken stock to make a light coating consistency.

Preheat the oven to moderate (180 c, 350 f, gas 4).

Soften the tortillas on a griddle or fry in lard or oil only long enough to wilt them. Dunk them in the sauce, turning over to coat well. As they are ready, fill each one with some chicken meat, roll up and arrange in a greased baking dish (a big, oval one) in one layer. If there's any sauce left over, dilute it with a bit more stock and pour over the filled *enchiladas*. Spread on the cream and sprinkle with the cheese. Bake for 20–30 minutes or until well heated through and bubbly on top. Garnish with shredded lettuce and radishes cut to resemble flowers. Serve at once or the garnish will go soggy and the enchiladas will be limp.

If you want to prepare ahead of time, take the recipe up to the stage of filling and rolling up the *enchiladas*. Then set aside, or refrigerate. When ready to bake, pour over any remaining sauce, cover with cream and cheese and then bake for 30–40 minutes. Can also be frozen.

Chilaquiles bravos

CHILAQUILES WITH RED CHILLI AND TOMATO SAUCE

METRIC/IMPERIAL

50 g/2 oz dried chillies, either *guajillos* (VERY hot), *pasilla* (fairly hot) or *ancho* – or a mixture – or 4 tablespoons chilli powder

2–3 large tomatoes (about 400 g/14 oz), or 1 400-g/14-oz can peeled tomatoes

1 onion, peeled

1 clove garlic

1 tablespoon lard or oil

salt

1 litre/1¾ pints stock

3 eggs, lightly beaten

12–16 stale tortillas, torn in pieces, fried till crisp and drained

wafer-thin onion rings

plain yogurt or sour cream

lime wedges

AMERICAN

2 oz dried chilies, either *guajillos* (VERY hot), *pasilla* (fairly hot) or *ancho* – or a mixture – or ¼ cup chili powder

2–3 large tomatoes (about 14 oz), or 1 16-oz can peeled tomatoes

1 onion, peeled

1 clove garlic

1 tablespoon lard or oil

salt

1 quart stock

3 eggs, lightly beaten

12–16 stale tortillas, torn into pieces, fried till crisp and drained

wafer-thin onion rings

plain yogurt or sour cream

lime wedges

Open up the chillies – using scissors or a knife or your fingers will smart for days – and remove the seeds and stalks. Heat through on a griddle or in a heavy, ungreased frying pan until supple and giving off a gently toasted smell. Do not let the chillies burn or they will give the sauce an acrid taste, and only toast the outside or you will nearly choke to death from the fumes. Soak in hot water for about 30 minutes while you do the rest.

Grill [broil] (or toast on the same griddle) the fresh tomatoes, onion and garlic until soft and lightly toasted. Peel the garlic. Blend the garlic, tomatoes, onion and drained chillies to a smooth purée in a food processor or blender. (If using canned tomatoes and chilli powder, blend them with the other ingredients.) Sieve, then fry in the lard or oil for about 10 minutes, adding salt to taste and stirring, until thick, syrupy and a nice dark brick-red. Dilute to a coating consistency with the stock and check seasoning.

When the sauce reaches a simmer again, scramble in the eggs and cook for a further 5 minutes, or just enough to set the egg. Finally, throw in the fried tortilla pieces and simmer over gentle heat until the liquid is absorbed and the tortillas are soft but not mushy. Or, if you prefer, you can bake the *chilaquiles* in the oven preheated to moderate (180 c, 350 F, gas 4) for 25 minutes.

To serve, arrange the onion rings in concentric circles over the top of the finished dish, and pour a bit of yogurt or sour cream into the middle. Serve the rest of the yogurt or sour cream in a separate dish, plus lime wedges for each person to serve with their *chilaquiles* (lime is wonderfully soothing for scorched tongues, as is yogurt or sour cream).

If you want to prepare this dish in advance, make the chilli sauce and fry the tortillas, and put aside at that stage. Then when you are ready to go ahead, scramble in the eggs, add the tortilla pieces and cook as directed. It all gets a bit soggy if you do the whole thing in advance.

Chilaquiles iniciados

CHILAQUILES WITH CREAMY GREEN SAUCE

METRIC/IMPERIAL
12–16 stale tortillas, torn in pieces
3–4 tablespoons lard or oil
1 425-g/15-oz can Mexican green tomatoes,
  drained, or 500 g/1 lb fresh green
  tomatoes or gooseberries
2–3 fresh green chillies
salt
handful of fresh coriander
1 small onion, peeled and chopped
1 clove garlic, peeled and crushed
250 ml/8 fl oz evaporated milk or single
  cream
75 g/3 oz Cheddar cheese, grated

AMERICAN
12–16 stale tortillas, torn into pieces
3–4 tablespoons lard or oil
1 16-oz can Mexican green tomatoes,
  drained, or 1 lb fresh green tomatoes or
  gooseberries
2–3 fresh green chilies
salt
handful of fresh coriander
1 small onion, peeled and chopped
1 clove garlic, peeled and minced
1 cup evaporated milk or light cream
¾ cup grated Cheddar cheese

Fry the tortilla pieces in the hot lard or oil until pale golden. Drain on paper towels.

If using fresh green tomatoes, remove husks (or top and tail gooseberries) and simmer with the chillies and salt to taste, with water just to cover, for about 10 minutes: they should not be too soft, and should not burst open. Drain and blend in a food processor or blender (adding canned tomatoes here, if relevant) with the coriander, onion, garlic and milk or cream until smooth.

Heat the same pan you used to fry the tortilla pieces, adding a little more fat if necessary to make about 1 tablespoonful. Add the sauce and fry until well-seasoned and thick, stirring from time to time. Add a little water or stock if necessary to make a lightly coating consistency.

Shortly before serving, drop in the tortilla pieces and simmer gently for 10–15 minutes or until they have absorbed almost all the sauce. Sprinkle on the grated cheese and put briefly under a preheated grill [broiler] to melt the cheese.

Right top: *sincronizadas* (page 81); bottom: *pastes pachuqueños* (page 84)
Overleaf clockwise, from the top: *calabacitas rancheras* (page 153), *arroz blanco* (page 143), *pescado con almendra y ajonjolí* (page 88), *calamares a la veracruzana* (page 94)

Chilaquiles rojos

RED CHILAQUILES IN SPICY TOMATO SAUCE

METRIC/IMPERIAL	AMERICAN
12–16 stale tortillas, cut in wedges	12–16 stale tortillas, cut into wedges
3–4 tablespoons lard or oil	3–4 tablespoons lard or oil
1 quantity *caldillo de jitomate* (see page 36)	1 quantity *caldillo de jitomate* (see page 36)
3–4 eggs, lightly beaten	3–4 eggs, lightly beaten
125 g/4 oz crumbly fresh cheese	¼ lb crumbly fresh cheese
2 tablespoons finely chopped onion	2 tablespoons finely chopped onion
250 ml/8 fl oz sour cream or plain yogurt	1 cup sour cream or plain yogurt

Fry the tortilla pieces in the hot lard or oil until pale golden and slightly crisp. Drain on paper towels.

Shortly before serving, throw the fried tortillas into the simmering sauce, add the eggs and cook gently, stirring from time to time, until nice and hot, the eggs are set and the sauce has been absorbed by the tortilla pieces. Sprinkle on the crumbled cheese, scatter on the onion and pour on a pool of sour cream or yogurt in the middle.

Left *arroz con mariscos* (page 95)

TACOS

Illustrated on pages 50–51

The name *taco* is a fairly loose term which covers a multitude of sins (the very worst of which is committed in package form and comes with an instant seasoning mix). In real Mexican life, however, there are two main sorts: *tacos suaves*, or warm tortillas straight from the griddle or basket, filled (on the hand), rolled up and eaten without further ado; and secondly *tacos dorados*, where the tortillas are filled, rolled up, secured with toothpicks and fried till golden and crispy.

The first sort are great for an informal party: make up a selection of *taco* fillings and have them dotted about, maybe keeping warm on spirit burners, and a big cloth-lined basket of steaming tortillas in the middle (a bit like a fondue party). Each guest takes a tortilla, fills it, adds a dollop of sauce, rolls it up and eats instantly. Discourage fancy ideas like plates, knives and forks: this is the best sort of hand-to-mouth food which will get cold and leathery on a plate, and won't taste at all the same at a knife-and-fork's length, though an industrial supply of napkins helps a lot.

The second variety, the fried *tacos*, are better if you're looking for something that can be prepared a little in advance. Most of the fillings which follow can be used for either version, and more ideas follow with the *tortillas de harina* (wheat tortillas) on page 78. They're all lovely, and should be served with any of the table sauces in the Sauces chapter, though *guacamole* and *salsa mexicana* are sort of mandatory.

Each filling should be enough for about 12 tortillas.

Tacos de rajas

TACOS WITH CREAMY CHILLI, PEPPER AND ONION FILLING

METRIC/IMPERIAL	AMERICAN
4 green peppers	4 sweet green peppers
2–3 fresh green chillies or canned *chiles jalapeños*	2–3 fresh green chilies or canned *chiles jalapeños*
1 tablespoon oil or lard	1 tablespoon oil or lard
1 large onion, peeled and sliced	1 large onion, peeled and sliced
salt and pepper	salt and pepper
250 ml/8 fl oz double cream or *crème fraiche*	1 cup heavy cream or *crème fraiche*
150 g/5 oz Cheddar cheese, grated	1¼ cups grated Cheddar cheese

Follow the detailed instructions for grilling [broiling] and peeling peppers in the recipe for *chiles rellenos de queso* (see page 54), but instead of leaving them whole, tear them in strips (*rajas*) about 5 mm/¼ inch wide. Cut the chillies also into very thin lengthwise strips and discard seeds if you're heat-sensitive. Heat the oil or lard in a heavy frying pan and soften the onion without browning. Add the pepper and chilli strips, and salt and pepper to taste and continue cooking, covered, until soft (about 10 minutes). Stir in the cream and grated cheese and cook until the cheese melts. Use to fill the tacos.

Tacos de picadillo

TACOS WITH MINCED MEAT, NUTS AND FRUIT

METRIC/IMPERIAL	AMERICAN
1 medium onion, peeled and chopped	1 medium-size onion, peeled and chopped
1 clove garlic, peeled and crushed	1 clove garlic, peeled and minced
1 tablespoon oil	1 tablespoon oil
250 g/8 oz minced pork	½ lb ground pork
250 g/8 oz minced beef	½ lb ground beef
3 large tomatoes (about 500 g/1 lb), peeled and chopped	3 large tomatoes (about 1 lb), peeled and chopped
1 bay leaf	1 bay leaf
pinch of ground cinnamon	pinch of ground cinnamon
salt and pepper	salt and pepper
50 g/2 oz blanched almonds, chopped	½ cup chopped blanched almonds
50 g/2 oz raisins	⅓ cup raisins
25 g/1 oz chopped candied peel	3 tablespoons chopped candied peel

Soften the onion and garlic in the oil without browning, then raise the heat, add the meats and fry until lightly browned. Tip out any excess fat. Add the tomatoes, bay leaf, cinnamon, and salt and pepper to taste and continue cooking till the juices are almost evaporated. Stir in the almonds, raisins and peel and cook a few minutes more. Use to fill the tacos.

Tacos de pollo

TACOS WITH CHICKEN FILLING

These are nearly always served fried as *tacos dorados*.

METRIC/IMPERIAL	AMERICAN
500 g/1 lb cooked chicken meat, shredded	1 lb cooked chicken meat, shredded (2–2½ cups)
salt and pepper	salt and pepper
lard or oil	lard or oil
sour cream	sour cream
shredded lettuce	shredded lettuce
chopped onion	chopped onion

Fill the softened tortillas with the well-seasoned chicken. Roll up, secure with wooden toothpicks and fry in hot lard or oil until golden and crispy. Drain on paper towels, then daub on some sour cream, sprinkle on lettuce and onion, and serve.

Pastel delicia

LAYERED TORTILLA PIE WITH CHICKEN, HAM
AND CORN FILLING

This is good for a quick family supper after a lightning raid on the cupboards, refrigerator and freezer. It's one of the very few occasions when I have to concede (reluctantly) that even canned tortillas would do, though they really are emergency rations.

METRIC/IMPERIAL
1 large onion, peeled and thinly sliced
2 75-g/3-oz cans peeled green chillies (mild), or 2–3 *chiles jalapeños en escabeche* (scorchers), drained and cut in strips
1 tablespoon lard or oil
1 400-g/14-oz can peeled tomatoes
salt and pepper
12 tortillas, preferably stale
250 g/8 oz cooked chicken meat, shredded
250 g/8 oz cooked or canned ham, cut in strips
200 g/7 oz corn kernels, canned or frozen, drained or thawed
250 ml/8 fl oz evaporated milk or single cream
125 g/4 oz Cheddar cheese, grated

AMERICAN
1 large onion, peeled and thinly sliced
2 3-oz cans peeled green chilies (mild), or 2–3 *chiles jalapeños en escabeche* (scorchers), drained and cut into strips
1 tablespoon lard or oil
1 16-oz can peeled tomatoes
salt and pepper
12 tortillas, preferably stale
½ lb cooked chicken meat, shredded (about 1 cup)
½ lb cooked or canned ham, cut into strips (about 1 cup)
1 cup whole kernel corn, canned or frozen, drained or thawed
1 cup evaporated milk or light cream
1 cup grated Cheddar cheese

Preheat the oven to moderate (180 c, 350 f, gas 4).

Soften the onion and chilli strips in the lard or oil without browning. Raise the heat and add the tomatoes, plus their juice. Season with the salt and pepper and cook hard, mashing and mixing, until the juice is somewhat evaporated: you don't want your filling to be a watery, soggy mess.

Using a round ovenproof dish about 20 cm/8 inches in diameter and 6 cm/2½ inches deep, place three tortillas in the bottom, fanning them out and overlapping slightly. Spread on some of the tomato/chilli sauce then sprinkle on some chicken, ham, corn, a little milk or cream and some cheese. Continue in this way until all the ingredients are used up, finishing up with some milk or cream and cheese.

Bake for 25–35 minutes or until golden brown and bubbly and heated right through. Serve with a green salad.

Budín azteca

LAYERED TORTILLA PIE WITH MEAT, TOMATO SAUCE,
CREAM AND CHEESE

A slightly up-market version of the preceding recipe, this makes a tasty, colourful dish – great for a party. If you substitute wheat tortillas for corn ones, it becomes a *budín norteño*.

METRIC/IMPERIAL	AMERICAN
1 large chicken, or 750 g/1½ lb piece boneless pork shoulder	1 large chicken, or 1½ lb piece boneless pork shoulder roast
3 onions, peeled and 2 thinly sliced	3 onions, peeled and 2 thinly sliced
1 clove garlic, peeled	1 clove garlic, peeled
1 carrot, peeled	1 carrot, peeled
herbs to taste	herbs to taste
salt and pepper	salt and pepper
4 green peppers	4 sweet green peppers
1 tablespoon oil or lard	1 tablespoon oil or lard
20–24 tortillas	20–24 tortillas
2 quantities *caldillo de jitomate* (see page 36)	2 quantities *caldillo de jitomate* (see page 36)
kernels from 2 large corn cobs, or 400 g/14 oz frozen corn kernels	kernels from 2 large ears of corn, or 14 oz (about 2¾ cups) frozen whole kernel corn
250 ml/8 fl oz double cream or *crème fraiche*	1 cup heavy cream or *crème fraiche*
50 g/2 oz Cheddar cheese, grated	½ cup grated Cheddar cheese

Simmer the chicken or pork in water to cover with the whole onion, garlic, carrot, and herbs, salt and pepper to taste until just tender. Cool, then drain, remove the meat from the bones and shred it.

Grill [broil] and peel the peppers according to the instructions in *chiles rellenos de queso* (see page 54). Cut in thin strips. Soften the sliced onions in the oil or lard without browning, then add the pepper strips, and salt and pepper to taste and cook 5 minutes more. You should now have an array of prepared ingredients ready for assembly: tortillas, cooked and shredded meat, tomato sauce, and the onion/pepper mixture. To make in advance, prepare up to this point.

Preheat the oven to moderate (180 c, 350 f, gas 4) about an hour before you plan to serve the pie.

Using a large (25 cm/10 inch diameter) ovenproof dish, place 6 tortillas in a slightly overlapping circle in the bottom. Add some sauce, meat, peppers, corn, cream and cheese. Continue in this way until the ingredients have been used up, finishing with some cream and cheese. Pour around any remaining sauce and bake in the preheated oven for about 45 minutes, or until golden and bubbly and the cheese has melted. *Serves 8–10.*

Tortillas de harina

WHEAT TORTILLAS

Illustrated on pages 50–51

Wheat tortillas come from the north of Mexico, where they are preferred to the corn ones.

METRIC/IMPERIAL	AMERICAN
500 g/1 lb unbleached or plain flour	4 cups all-purpose flour
125 g/4 oz white vegetable shortening	½ cup shortening
2 teaspoons salt	2 teaspoons salt
250 ml/8 fl oz hand-hot water	1¼ cups hand-hot water

Mix together (or process using the plastic blade of a food processor) the flour, shortening and salt, as if making pastry. Add the water to make a smooth, supple dough which does not stick to your hands or working surface. Divide the dough into golf ball-sized pieces.

Heat a large griddle or heavy frying pan. Roll out one piece of dough with a lightly floured rolling pin as thinly as you can on an unfloured pastry slab, rotating the pin (rather than the tortilla) at each roll so as to get an even circle, about 15 cm/6 inches in diameter. Peel the tortilla off the working surface and lay it on the preheated griddle or pan. You should hear a slightly protesting sizzle and in 60 seconds it should have puffed up and be done on one side. Flip it over, cook the other side, then stack up on plate, covered with a dish towel to keep warm.

Continue in this way until all the tortillas are made. They will keep 4–5 days in the refrigerator in a plastic bag, and freeze well. *Makes about 30.*

BURRITOS

WHEAT TORTILLAS WITH VARIOUS FILLINGS

Burritos are to wheat tortillas what *tacos* are to corn ones: a hot, supple, tortilla is filled with something yummy, given a dollop of sauce, rolled or folded over and eaten with a minimum of ceremony. The fillings which follow, specifically for wheat tortillas, should each be enough for 10 tortillas. Of course, any of the taco fillings could be substituted, and the same comments about them making marvellous informal party food apply: make up a basket of them, plus a selection of fillings keeping warm on spirit burners or hotplates, scatter around a few sauces and lots of paper napkins, and tell everyone to help themselves.

Queso fundido

MELTED CHEESE FILLING

METRIC/IMPERIAL
500 g/1 lb Cheddar or other quick-melting, non-stringy cheese, grated
1 chorizo sausage (about 125 g/4 oz), skinned, crumbled and fried, or strips of fresh green chilli, or finely chopped, peeled tomato (optional)

AMERICAN
4 cups grated Cheddar or other quick-melting, non-stringy cheese
1 chorizo sausage (about ¼ lb), skinned, crumbled and fried, or strips of fresh green chili, or finely chopped, peeled tomato (optional)

Melt the cheese in a heavy pot over gentle heat, or use a fondue pot over a spirit burner. Add the chorizo, chilli strips or tomato, if used. As soon as the cheese melts, grab a warm tortilla from the basket, scoop in some cheese, add some sauce (of your choice), fold over and eat immediately.

Mochomos

CRISP-FRIED SHREDDED BEEF FILLING

METRIC/IMPERIAL	AMERICAN
625 g/1¼ lb chuck steak	1¼ lb chuck steak
1 onion, peeled	1 onion peeled
1 clove garlic, peeled	1 clove garlic, peeled
2 teaspoons salt	2 teaspoons salt
2 tablespoons lard or oil	2 tablespoons lard or oil

Barely cover the meat with water, add the onion, garlic and salt and simmer for about 2 hours or until tender. Drain.

Shred the meat finely with fingers or forks (it must be the sort of cut that will fall apart in strips). Heat the lard or oil and fry the meat till really golden and crispy. Use to fill the tortillas.

Frijól y queso

BEAN AND CHEESE FILLING

METRIC/IMPERIAL	AMERICAN
500 g/1 lb cooked pinto beans with their liquid, or 1 400-g/14-oz can pinto beans	1 lb cooked pinto beans with their liquid (about 2 cups), or 1 16-oz can pinto beans
1 tablespoon oil or lard	1 tablespoon oil or lard
125 g/4 oz Cheddar or raclette cheese, grated	1 cup grated Cheddar or raclette cheese

Purée the beans with some of their liquid in a blender or food processor. Heat the oil or lard to almost smoking and fry the purée, stirring hard, (it's apt to plop about rather) until in a fairly thick paste. Season to taste with salt and pepper and stir in the cheese, cooking until just melted. Use to fill the tortillas.

Huevos revueltos con chorizo

SCRAMBLED EGG AND SAUSAGE FILLING

Illustrated on pages 50–51

METRIC/IMPERIAL
350 g/12 oz chorizo or pure pork sausage, skinned and crumbled
2 large tomatoes (about 350 g/12 oz), peeled and chopped
2 small fresh green chillies, finely chopped (optional)
salt
4 eggs, lightly beaten

AMERICAN
¾ lb chorizo or pure pork link sausages, skinned and crumbled
2 large tomatoes (about ¾ lb), peeled and chopped
2 small fresh green chilies, finely chopped (optional)
salt
4 eggs, lightly beaten

Fry the crumbled sausage until golden and the fat rendered. Add the tomatoes and chillies, if used, and season with salt. Cook till the juices evaporate and the mixture is quite dry. Pour in the eggs and cook until just set, stirring occasionally. Use to fill the tortillas.

Sincronizadas

'SYNCHRONIZED' WHEAT TORTILLA SANDWICHES
WITH HAM AND CHEESE

Illustrated on page 69

These are marvellous for a quick supper. In Mexico we were spoilt and could buy wheat tortillas in any supermarket, but if you have a little nest of them in the freezer for just such a dish, you'll never be stuck. For each *sincronizada* you need:

METRIC/IMPERIAL
1 slice cooked ham the size of the tortillas
2 slices Cheddar or other quick-melting cheese
2 wheat tortillas

AMERICAN
1 slice cooked ham the size of the tortillas
2 slices Cheddar or other quick-melting cheese
2 wheat tortillas

Sandwich the ham and cheese between the two tortillas. Get a griddle or heavy, ungreased frying pan really hot, then toast the *sincronizada* well on both sides, pressing down with a spatula so the cheese melts and the tortillas are hot but not too frazzled. Cut in quarters and serve with *guacamole* or *salsa mexicana* (see page 34).

Huevos rancheros

FRIED EGGS WITH BEANS AND TOMATO SAUCE

This simple, tasty affair consisting of a tortilla topped with a fried egg, hot sauce and pot beans makes a super brunch dish or a quick supper. For each serving you need:

METRIC/IMPERIAL	AMERICAN
1 corn tortilla	1 corn tortilla
lard or oil for frying	lard or oil for frying
1 egg	1 egg
2–3 tablespoons *caldillo de jitomate* (see page 36)	2–3 tablespoons *caldillo de jitomate* (see page 36)
½ ladleful (about 120ml/4floz) *frijoles de olla* (see page 140)	½ ladleful (about ½ cup) *frijoles de olla* (see page 140)
2–3 dollops sour cream or plain yogurt	2–3 dollops sour cream or plain yogurt

Warm a plate in the oven. Fry the tortilla in hot lard or oil and put in the oven to keep warm. Fry the egg, place on the tortilla and pour over the hot sauce. Surround with the beans and spoon on the cream or yogurt.

Huevos en rabo de mestiza

EGGS POACHED IN SPICY TOMATO SAUCE

METRIC/IMPERIAL	AMERICAN
250ml/8floz stock	1 cup stock
1 quantity *caldillo de jitomate* (see page 36)	1 quantity *caldillo de jitomate* (see page 36)
6 eggs	6 eggs
4 tablespoons double cream or *crème fraiche* (optional)	¼ cup thick cream or *crème fraiche* (optional)
125g/4oz Cheddar cheese, grated	1 cup grated Cheddar cheese
hot tortillas to serve	hot tortillas for serving

Add the stock to the tomato sauce in a wide pan (with room enough to poach the six eggs). Bring to simmering point, then break in the eggs carefully and cook until just set. Lift out with some of their sauce, using a ladle, into hot soup bowls. Spoon on the cream, if used, sprinkle on the grated cheese and serve with hot tortillas. If you prefer, you can heat the sauce in an ovenproof dish, add the cream and cheese and bake in a preheated moderate oven (180 c, 350 f, gas 4) until the eggs are just set.

Huevos revueltos a la mexicana

MEXICAN SCRAMBLED EGGS

METRIC/IMPERIAL
½ quantity *caldillo de jitomate*, i.e. about
  250 ml/8 fl oz sauce (see page 36)
6 eggs
salt and pepper
tortilla chips, or crisply fried strips of stale
  tortilla (optional)

AMERICAN
½ quantity *caldillo de jitomate*, i.e. about 1
  cup sauce (see page 36)
6 eggs
salt and pepper
tortilla chips, or crisply-fried strips of stale
  tortilla (optional)

Make up the tomato sauce in the usual way, but using a nonstick frying pan
or saucepan. Beat the eggs lightly and season with salt and pepper, then tip
into the simmering sauce. Cook, stirring, until lightly scrambled. In Mexico
they are always cooked until rather dry and rubbery, but I prefer them a bit on
the creamy side. Stir in the tortilla pieces, if used, and serve immediately on
warm plates.

Molletes

FRENCH BREAD SPREAD WITH BEAN PURÉE AND CHEESE

My children's favourite supper, this is very quick to assemble, especially if
you just happen to have some bean purée loafing around.

METRIC/IMPERIAL
thick slices French bread or crusty rolls,
  cut in half
frijoles refritos (see page 140)
slices Cheddar cheese

AMERICAN
thick slices French bread or crusty
  biscuits, cut in half
frijoles refritos (see page 140)
slices Cheddar cheese

Spread the bread with the bean purée, top each slice with a slice of cheese and
brown quickly under a hot grill [broiler] till the cheese melts and the bread is
lightly toasted.

Pastes pachuqueños

SPICY PASTIES [TURNOVERS] FROM PACHUCA

Illustrated on page 69

This curious recipe comes from Pachuca, a small town in northeastern Mexico which saw a big influx of Cornish miners during the last century. A quick look at the ingredients will tell you that these are just 'chillified' Cornish pasties, which can be bought in any *panadería* in Pachuca, still with their English name.

METRIC/IMPERIAL	AMERICAN
400 g/14 oz plain flour	3½ cups all-purpose flour
salt and pepper	salt and pepper
2 teaspoons baking powder	2 teaspoons baking powder
250 g/8 oz butter or margarine	1 cup butter or margarine
1 egg mixed with enough cold water or milk to make up to 250 ml/8 fl oz	1 egg mixed with enough cold water or milk to make 1¼ cups
500 g/1 lb steak (the best you can afford), cut into small cubes	1 lb steak (the best you can afford), cut into small cubes
2 tablespoons finely chopped parsley	2 tablespoons finely chopped parsley
500 g/1 lb waxy potatoes, peeled and cubed	1 lb waxy potatoes, peeled and cubed
1 large onion, peeled and finely chopped	1 large onion, peeled and finely chopped
2–3 fresh green chillies, seeded and cut in rings	2–3 fresh green chilies, seeded and cut into rings
beaten egg to glaze	beaten egg for glaze

Make up the pastry with the flour, 1 teaspoon salt, the baking powder, butter or margarine, and egg and water mixture in the usual way, then chill.

Season the steak with salt and pepper and roll in the chopped parsley. Mix with the potatoes, onion, chillies and salt to taste.

Roll out the pastry and cut out 15 cm/6 inch discs. Fill with the meat mixture. Dampen the edges and fold over, pressing to seal well. Place on a lightly buttered baking sheet and brush with beaten egg. Bake for about 10 minutes to get them good and golden; then lower the heat to moderate (170 c, 325 f, gas 3) and bake for a further hour to cook through. *Makes about 14.*

TAMALES DE CAZUELA

TAMAL PIES

Delicious pies can be made using a *tamal* dough (see *tamales* in the vegetable chapter, page 135) to enclose a filling of meat and sauce, which is juicily sealed inside. In certain parts of Mexico such pies would be baked in a pit; in other areas they would be parcelled up in a banana leaf and baked on the fire. They make extremely satisfying, savoury pies and do particularly well for buffets, baked in a huge, colourful earthenware dish (even if your equipment doesn't run to pits or banana leaves).

Tamal de cazuela estilo casero

CHICKEN AND PORK BAKED IN TAMAL DOUGH

This is the best buffet dish of the lot!

METRIC/IMPERIAL	AMERICAN
1 chicken, cut into serving pieces	1 chicken, cut into serving pieces
750 g/1½ lb boned pork shoulder, cubed	1½ lb boneless pork shoulder, cubed
salt	salt
1 bay leaf	1 bay leaf
black peppercorns	black peppercorns
1 onion, peeled	1 onion, peeled
1 clove garlic, peeled	1 clove garlic, peeled
300 g/11 oz lard	1½ cups lard
500 g/1 lb *tortilla* flour	4 cups *tortilla* flour
100 g/4 oz plain white flour	1 cup all-purpose flour
700 ml/1 pint 4 fl oz hand-hot water	3 cups hand-hot water
2 teaspoons baking powder	2 teaspoons baking powder
1 quantity *caldillo de jitomate* (see page 36), made with a pinch of aniseed	1 quantity *caldillo de jitomate* (see page 36), made with a pinch of aniseed
plain yogurt	plain yogurt
4 green peppers, grilled, peeled and cut in strips	4 green peppers, grilled, peeled and cut in strips
6 green chillies, cut in strips	6 green chilies, cut in strips
100 g/4 oz crumbly white cheese	1 cup crumbly white cheese

Cover the chicken pieces and cubes of pork with water, add salt to taste, the bay leaf, peppercorns, onion and garlic and simmer till just tender (30–40 minutes – the chicken will be cooked first). Cool a little, then drain, reserving the stock, and take the chicken meat off the bone. Strain the stock and reserve 250 ml/8 fl oz [1 cup].

Preheat the oven to moderate (180 c, 350 f, gas 4).

In an electric mixer, cream the lard until light and fluffy (as if making a cake). It will become quite white and look like whipped cream. Meanwhile, mix the two flours and the hot water to make a tortilla dough in the usual way. Add the reserved meat stock. Drop this dough by spoonsful into the mixer with the lard, continuing to beat, and add the baking powder and about 1 tablespoons salt. The resulting dough should be really light and fluffy, and a ball of it dropped into a cup of cold water should float.

Spread about two-thirds of this dough over the bottom and up the sides of an ovenproof dish about 25 cm/10 inches wide and 10 cm/4 inches deep. Mix the meats with the tomato sauce and put them in the dough case. Spread over the rest of the dough to seal it all in, then bake for 1–1½ hours or until the top is golden brown and quite set. Serve hot, with small bowls of plain yogurt, strips of roasted and peeled green peppers and chillies, and grated or crumbled cheese, for everyone to help themselves. *Serves 10–12.*

Variations

You can use practically any of the chicken or pork dishes in sauce which figure in later chapters – you are limited only by your imagination. Bear in mind that for this quantity of dough, you need approximately 1.5 kg/3 lb of meat-with-sauce, and then make up your own personalized *tamal de cazuela*.

FISH

Inevitable that Mexico, with its thousands of kilometers of coastline on the Pacific and on the Gulf side, not to mention the Caribbean just round the corner, should have an unlimited supply of fresh fish and shellfish, and an unlimited choice of recipes to match. Trying to choose just a few for this section was hard, but I've tried to stick to those that are original, feasible for non-Mexican households as well as delicious.

Incidentally, the Mexicans are generally about as conservative as we are about trying out new and unfamiliar fish (not to mention fish that actually has a recognizable head and bones), tending to concentrate rather heavily on red snapper and pompano, at the expense of many other delicious fish. You can use haddock or really fresh cod to great advantage in any of these dishes, but why not take a leaf out of the French housewife's book and try out as big a variety of fresh fish as we can get. Bother your fishmonger (if you're lucky enough to have one), ask him what's good and fresh at the moment, ask him what HE eats for his supper. If he doesn't seem interested, or worse, quite obviously finds you rather a bore, change your fishmonger.

Pescado almendrado	Fish in an almond crust
Pescado con almendra y ajonjolí	Fish with creamy almond and sesame seed sauce
Pescado en salsa verde	Fish in a creamy green pepper sauce
Pescado en naranja	Fish with orange marinade
Calamares a la veracruzana	Squid in tomato sauce with olives
Pescado en salsa de avellanas	Fish in hazelnut sauce
Arroz con mariscos	Seafood pilaff

Pescado almendrado

FISH BAKED IN AN ALMOND CRUST

METRIC/IMPERIAL

6–8 steaks or fillets of any firm, white fish,
  or 1 whole fish weighing about 1.5 kg/3 lb
  (cleaned weight)
salt
lime juice
2 large tomatoes (about 350 g/12 oz)
6 black peppercorns
2 cloves
1 bay leaf
150 g/5 oz unblanched almonds
2 tablespoons oil
2 slices French bread, cubed

AMERICAN

6–8 steaks or fillets of any firm, white fish,
  or 1 whole fish weighing about 3 lb
  (cleaned weight)
salt
lime juice
2 large tomatoes (about $\frac{3}{4}$ lb)
6 black peppercorns
2 cloves
1 bay leaf
1$\frac{1}{3}$ cups unblanched almonds
2 tablespoons oil
2 slices French bread, cubed

Season the fish with salt and lime juice and set aside to marinate while you prepare the almond paste.

Preheat the oven to moderate (180 c, 350 f, gas 4).

Grill [broil] the tomatoes until soft and blistered; toast the peppercorns, cloves and bay leaf gently on a griddle. Place all these ingredients in a blender or food processor. Fry the almonds in the hot oil until nicely toasted, and add to the blender. Do the same with the bread cubes. Blend all to a fairly smooth paste, adding salt to taste and a little water only if the blades can't cope – you may need to do quite a bit of pushing down with a spatula.

Place a layer of the paste in a shallow ovenproof dish. Place the fish on top and spread over the rest of the paste so that the fish is completely covered. Bake for about 30 minutes, basting occasionally with the juices, until the almond paste is slightly crusty and the fish just cooked. Serve with *arroz verde* (rice with green peppers – see page 145) and *acelgas con crema* (chard with cream sauce – see page 156).

Pescado con almendra y ajonjolí

FISH WITH ALMOND AND SESAME SEED SAUCE

Illustrated on pages 70–71

A quickly prepared, delicate, pale green, creamy fish dish.

METRIC/IMPERIAL
6–8 steaks or fillets of any firm, white fish
salt and pepper
lime or lemon juice
2 slices crustless bread, cubed (about
  50 g/2 oz)
50 g/2 oz blanched almonds
2 tablespoons sesame seeds
2 tablespoons oil
4 lettuce leaves, or 4 tablespoons chopped
  parsley
2 tablespoons capers or finely chopped
  gherkins
2 fresh or canned green chillies, seeded
1 small clove garlic, peeled and crushed
1 small onion, peeled and chopped
about 250 ml/8 fl oz fish stock, or half white
  wine and half water

AMERICAN
6–8 steaks or fillets of any firm, white fish
salt and pepper
lime or lemon juice
2 slices crustless bread, cubed
½ cup blanched almonds
2 tablespoons sesame seeds
2 tablespoons oil
4 lettuce leaves, or ¼ cup chopped parsley
2 tablespoons capers or finely chopped
  gherkins
2 fresh or canned green chilies, seeded
1 small clove garlic, peeled and minced
1 small onion, peeled and chopped
about 1 cup fish stock, or half white wine
  and half water

Season the fish with salt, pepper and lime or lemon juice. Set aside to marinate while you prepare the sauce.

Fry the bread cubes, almonds and sesame seeds in 1 tablespoon oil until golden. Blend to a powder in a blender or food processor, then add the remaining ingredients and blend again, adding a little fish stock (or wine and water) only if necessary to release the blades. Reheat the oil (add more if the bread soaked it all up) in the same pan and fry the sauce, stirring well, until thick and tasty. Thin to a lightly coating consistency with more fish stock (or wine and water) and simmer for about 10 minutes to blend flavours and to be sure the onion and garlic are cooked.

Meanwhile, heat the remaining tablespoon of oil in another heavy frying pan and fry the fish briefly on both sides until just cooked. Transfer the fish to a warmed serving dish. Pour over the sauce and serve immediately, with any freshly cooked green vegetable and *arroz blanco* (white rice) in a ring mould – (see page 143).

Right *carne de puerco con piña* (page 103), served with courgettes
Overleaf *lengua almendrada* (page 116), served with white rice and corn kernels

Pescado en salsa verde

FISH IN A CREAMY GREEN PEPPER SAUCE WITH CORIANDER

METRIC/IMPERIAL	AMERICAN
6–8 steaks or fillets of any firm, white fish	6 steaks or fillets of any firm, white fish
salt and pepper	salt and pepper
lime juice	lime juice
4 green peppers	4 sweet green peppers
2 fresh green chillies	2 fresh green chilies
250 ml/8 fl oz double cream or *crème fraiche*	1 cup thick cream or *crème fraiche*
2 tablespoons chopped fresh coriander	2 tablespoons chopped fresh coriander

Season the fish with salt, pepper and lime juice and set aside to marinate while you prepare the sauce.

Preheat the oven to moderate (180 c, 350 f, gas 4).

Grill [broil] the peppers and chillies until charred and blistered. Peel the peppers and discard stalks and seeds. Seed (but don't attempt to peel, unless they are very large ones) the chillies and discard stalks. Blend together with the peppers and the remaining ingredients in a blender or food processor to a smooth sauce.

Spread a little sauce on the bottom of an ovenproof dish. Place the fish on top and add the rest of the sauce. Cover with foil and bake for 25–30 minutes or until the fish is just cooked. Serve with *papas con rajas* (spicy potatoes – see page 147) and a *torta de calabacitas* (baked courgette [zucchini] torte – see page 155).

Pescado en naranja

FISH IN ORANGE SAUCE

METRIC/IMPERIAL	AMERICAN
6–8 steaks or fillets of any firm, white fish	6–8 steaks or fillets of any firm, white fish
salt and pepper	salt and pepper
lime or lemon juice	lime or lemon juice
2 tablespoons olive oil	2 tablespoons olive oil
2 slices bread, cubed	2 slices bread, cubed
2 cloves garlic	2 cloves garlic
4 tablespoons chopped parsley	¼ cup chopped parsley
3 tablespoons salad oil	3 tablespoons salad oil
juice of 2 oranges	juice of 2 oranges

Preheat the oven to moderate (180 c, 350 f, gas 4).

Season the fish with salt, pepper and lime or lemon juice. Place in a lightly greased ovenproof dish.

Heat the olive oil and fry the bread cubes and garlic cloves until golden. Peel the garlic and blend with the bread cubes and the remaining ingredients, in a food processor or blender until smooth. Pour over the fish.

Bake for 25–30 minutes or until the fish is tender, basting with the juices occasionally. Serve with *frijoles veracruzanos* (black beans – see page 141) and a *budín de zanahoria* (carrot torte – see page 158).

Left *chorizo* (page 101) can be bought ready prepared or made at home

Calamares a la veracruzana

SQUID WITH TOMATO, CHILLI AND OLIVES

Illustrated on pages 70–71

METRIC/IMPERIAL
1 kg/2 lb whole squid (to give about
  400 g/14 oz when cleaned)
salt and pepper
2 tablespoons oil
1 medium onion, peeled and chopped
1 clove garlic, peeled and crushed
3 large tomatoes (about 500 g/1 lb), peeled,
  or 1 400-g/14-oz can tomatoes
4 fresh green chillies, cut in fine strips
mixed herbs to taste (parsley, oregano,
  thyme and bay leaf)
16 green olives
1 tablespoon capers

AMERICAN
2 lb whole squid (to give about 14 oz when
  cleaned)
salt and pepper
2 tablespoons oil
1 medium-size onion, peeled and chopped
1 clove garlic, peeled and minced
3 large tomatoes (about 1 lb), peeled, or 1
  16-oz can peeled tomatoes
4 fresh green chillies, cut into fine strips
mixed herbs to taste (parsley, oregano,
  thyme and bay leaf)
16 green olives
1 tablespoon capers

Empty out the squid and discard all the nasties, including the thin transparent backbone running down one side. You will be left with a series of cylindrical bodies which you should slice into rings. Dry a little on paper towels, season with salt and pepper and fry in hot oil until stiffened and opaque. Remove and keep warm.

Soften the onion and garlic in the same oil. Add the tomatoes, chillies, salt to taste and herbs, cover and cook slowly till the juice is rendered. Uncover the pan, raise the heat and cook until nice and thick. (Canned tomatoes will take longer than fresh because of their extra juice.)

Stir in the squid, olives and capers and simmer together for a further 5–10 minutes to blend the flavours. Serve inside a ring of *arroz blanco* (white rice) or *arroz verde* (see pages 143 and 145).

Pescado en salsa de avellanas

FISH IN HAZELNUT SAUCE

METRIC/IMPERIAL
6–8 steaks or fillets of any firm, white fish
1 onion, peeled and thinly sliced
1 stick celery, chopped
1 tablespoon vinegar
1 bay leaf
thyme
salt
SAUCE:
1 large slice crustless bread, cubed
125 g/4 oz hazelnuts
1 clove garlic
1 tablespoon oil
2 tablespoons chopped parsley
1 envelope (12 g/½ oz) powdered saffron
1 teaspoon salt

AMERICAN
6–8 steaks or fillets of any firm, white fish
1 onion, peeled and thinly sliced
1 stalk celery, chopped
1 tablespoon vinegar
1 bay leaf
thyme
salt
SAUCE:
1 large slice crustless bread, cubed
1 cup hazelnuts
1 clove garlic
1 tablespoon oil
2 tablespoons chopped parsley
1 envelope (½ oz) powdered saffron
1 teaspoon salt

Preheat the oven to moderate (180 c, 350 f, gas 4).

Place the fish in a lightly greased ovenproof dish. Add the onion, celery, vinegar, herbs and salt to taste, plus just enough water to cover. Cover with foil and bake for 20–25 minutes or until the fish is opaque. Drain, reserving the stock, and keep warm.

Fry the bread cubes, hazelnuts and garlic clove in the oil until golden. Peel the garlic and blend it together with the bread, hazelnuts, parsley, saffron, salt and 250 ml/8 fl oz [1 cup] of the reserved fish stock in a blender or food processor until smooth. Reheat the oil in the same pan and fry the sauce, stirring well, until thick and tasty. Thin down, if necessary, to a light coating consistency with more of the remaining stock.

Pour the sauce over the fish and serve immediately, with some plainly boiled tiny potatoes (in Mexico they would be the little pink ones), and some sliced plantains or bananas, lightly fried in lard or oil.

Arroz con mariscos

SEAFOOD PILAFF

Illustrated on page 72

METRIC/IMPERIAL
200 g/7 oz long-grain rice
2 medium tomatoes (about 250 g/8 oz)
1 clove garlic
1 onion, peeled
2 fresh green or red chillies (about 25 g/1 oz)
salt
about 350 ml/12 fl oz fish or chicken stock
2 tablespoons oil
250 g/8 oz mixed prepared shellfish (fresh, frozen or canned)
125 g/4 oz French beans, frozen or blanched fresh
plenty of chopped fresh coriander
1 avocado, peeled, stoned and cut in 8 segments

AMERICAN
1 cup long-grain rice
2 medium-size tomatoes (about ½ lb)
1 clove garlic
1 onion, peeled
2 fresh green or red chilies (about 1 oz)
salt
about 1½ cups fish or chicken stock
2 tablespoons oil
½ lb mixed prepared shellfish (fresh, frozen or canned)
¼ lb green beans, frozen or blanched fresh
plenty of chopped fresh coriander
1 avocado, peeled, seeded and cut into 8 segments

Soak the rice in hot water to cover while you get on with the rest.

Grill [broil] the tomatoes, garlic, onion and chillies until blistered and soft. Quarter the tomatoes and onion; remove seeds and stalks from the chillies; peel the garlic. Blend all together in a food processor or blender till smooth. Add salt to taste and enough stock to make up to about 450 ml/¾ pint [2 cups].

Drain, rinse and shake dry the rice. Heat the oil in a heavy flameproof casserole to near-smoking point (a grain dropped in will fizzle fiercely), throw in the rice and fry, stirring, over lively heat till golden, glistening and sticky-looking. Stir in the shellfish, beans and coriander, and add the tomato/stock mixture. Cover and cook gently for 20–25 minutes or until the rice has absorbed all the stock and is just tender but not mushy.

Garnish with the avocado slices, sprinkle with more coriander and serve with a sharply-dressed green salad.

PORK

Pork is the most commonly used meat in Mexican cooking, and doubtless because of the enormous demand and quick turnover, it's delicious. The butcher at the market stall where I used to buy all my pork would think nothing of bringing 300 kilos/660 pounds of pork to market, and in a single brisk morning's trading would dispose of it all. In most other parts of the world, pork is relegated to second best ('Poor piggy, when he's so delicious,' as Julia Child once remarked). I hope some of the following recipes will turn you into a puercophile.

Two points to note: firstly, a cut of pork that has some fat *and* lean will be juicier and tenderer than the wholly lean boned loin or tenderloin. Secondly, do resist the temptation to overcook pork – another reason for its reputation as a dry, dull meat. A reading of 71c/160f on a meat thermometer is quite enough, since the dreaded trichinae emitted their last gasp way back at 58c/137f.

Carne de puerco michoacana	Pork chops in tomato sauce
Chuletas adobadas	Pork chops in chilli marinade
Carne de puerco con chipotle	Pork with creamy smoked chilli sauce
Chiles en nogada	Peppers stuffed with minced pork, beef, fruit and nuts, walnut and cream sauce
Chorizo	Home-made spicy sausage cakes
Manchamantel	Pork and chicken in a red chilli sauce with nuts and fruit
Carne de pnerco con piña	Pork stew with red chillies and pineapple
Carne de puerco en chile verde	Pork in a creamy green pepper sauce
Carnitas	Crispy fried pork pieces
Lomo con chiles cuaresmeños rojos	Pork with red chilli, tomato and cream sauce

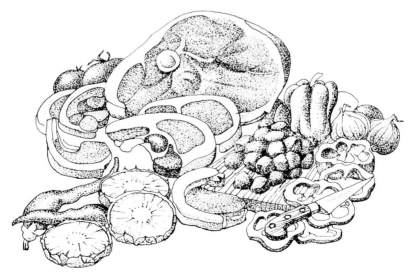

Carne de puerco michoacana

PORK CHOPS IN TOMATO SAUCE WITH TRIMMINGS

Illustrated on page 109

This system for cooking pork, which you will find in several of the recipes that follow, may strike non-Mexicans as 'back-to-front' – i.e. the meat is barely covered with water and cooked steadily until the liquid has evaporated and the meat fries in its own rendered fat. It's an excellent system for dealing with a not-too-lean cut of meat, which is cooked tender but crusty on the outside, without the addition of any extra fat. This recipe is adapted from Diana Kennedy's recipe *carne de puerco con uchepos*.

METRIC/IMPERIAL	AMERICAN
6 pork chops or steaks	6 pork chops or steaks
salt	salt
3 large tomatoes (about 500 g/1 lb)	3 large tomatoes (about 1 lb)
2 fresh green chillies	2 fresh green chilies
1 clove garlic	1 clove garlic
1 onion, peeled and quartered	1 onion, peeled and quartered
2 green peppers, grilled and peeled (see page 54), and cut in strips, or 1 75-g/3-oz can peeled green chillies, drained and cut in strips	2 sweet green peppers, broiled and peeled (see page 54), and cut into strips, or 1 3-oz can peeled green chilies, drained and cut into strips
250 ml/8 fl oz sour cream or plain yogurt	1 cup sour cream or plain yogurt
150 g/5 oz crumbly white cheese, or Cheddar cheese, grated	5 oz crumbly white cheese, or 1¼ cups grated Cheddar cheese

Put the meat, in one layer, in a wide, heavy flameproof casserole, barely cover with water and add salt to taste. Cook over medium heat until tender and the water has evaporated (30–40 minutes). The meat will start to fry in its own rendered fat, but be careful not to let it burn. Turn the chops once so they are evenly golden.

Remove the chops from the casserole and set aside. Pour off all but 1 tablespoon fat. (Don't attempt to use the same fat if it did burn: better to clean out the casserole and start afresh with 1 tablespoon lard for the next step.)

Grill [broil] the tomatoes, fresh chillies and garlic until blistered and soft. Quarter the tomatoes (don't peel, unless there are some really blackened bits: all the flavour and goodness is in the skin); seed the chillies if you're heat-sensitive; peel the garlic. Blend these three ingredients together with the onion and salt to taste in a food processor or blender. Push the sauce through a sieve or food mill.

Heat the reserved fat or lard in the casserole, throw in the strained sauce and fry until thick and syrupy, stirring from time to time. Place the chops in the sauce for a final communal simmer (about 10 minutes).

Arrange the chops with the sauce on a long serving dish. Garnish with the pepper or chilli strips, pour a little of the sour cream or yogurt around the edge and sprinkle on some of the cheese. Serve the rest of the cream and cheese separately. Serve with *uchepos* (fresh corn 'dumplings' – see page 138) and *frijoles refritos* (puréed and fried beans – see page 140).

Chuletas adobadas

PORK CHOPS IN CHILLI PASTE

Adobo (not to be confused with *adobe*, used for building houses) is a chilli paste which used to serve as a preservative in the days before refrigeration. It makes a useful and delicious marinade which seals in the juices and flavours the meat wonderfully.

METRIC/IMPERIAL
4 *chiles anchos*, or 4 tablespoons chilli powder
pinch of dried oregano
pinch of dried thyme
pinch of cumin seed
1-cm/½-in piece cinnamon stick
black peppercorns
2 large tomatoes (about 350 g/12 oz)
1 onion, peeled
2 cloves garlic
2 teaspoons salt
2 tablespoons white wine or cider vinegar
6 large pork chops, trimmed of fat
toasted breadcrumbs (optional)
oil or lard for frying
radish 'flowers'
wafer-thin onion rings

AMERICAN
4 *chiles anchos*, or ¼ cup chili powder
pinch of dried oregano
pinch of dried thyme
pinch of cumin seed
½ inch piece cinnamon stick
black peppercorns
2 large tomatoes (about ¾ lb)
1 onion, peeled
2 cloves garlic
2 teaspoons salt
2 tablespoons white wine or cider vinegar
6 large pork chops, trimmed of fat
toasted bread crumbs (optional)
oil or lard for frying
radish 'flowers'
wafer-thin onion rings

If using whole *chiles anchos*, soften them with the oregano, thyme, cumin, cinnamon and peppercorns on a griddle or in a heavy, ungreased frying pan until warm, supple and fragrant. Remove stalks and seeds from the chillies and tear in rough pieces. Cover with hot water and leave to soak for about 20 minutes or until floppy. Place the herbs and spices in a blender or food processor.

Toast or grill [broil] the tomatoes, onion and garlic. Quarter the tomatoes and onion; peel the garlic. Add to the blender or food processor with the drained chilli pieces (or chilli powder), salt and vinegar and blend to a smooth, thick paste.

Spread the paste on the chops. Leave them to marinate in a cool place or in the refrigerator for the flavours to permeate the meat (at least 6 hours, or more if you can).

When ready to cook, press a layer of breadcrumbs gently on to the paste, on both sides of the chops. Fry in hot oil or lard until golden and the chops are cooked through (or fry without breadcrumbs, if you prefer, although it's apt to be a bit messy). Garnish with radishes and onion rings and serve with one of the rice dishes.

Carne de puerco con chipotle

PORK WITH CREAMY SMOKED CHILLI SAUCE

The original recipe for this dish called for poached chicken breasts covered with this sauce, but I think pork has more character, especially when cooked in this way.

METRIC/IMPERIAL
750 g–1 kg/1½–2 lb boned roast of pork, with a combination of fat and lean
salt and pepper
herbs to taste
2 tablespoons lime or lemon juice
1 clove garlic, peeled and crushed
1–3 *chiles chipotles en adobo*, seeded (see Glossary)
250 ml/8 fl oz double cream or *crème fraiche*
50 g/2 oz mixed Parmesan and Gruyère cheeses, grated

AMERICAN
1½–2 lb boneless pork roast, with a combination of fat and lean
salt and pepper
herbs to taste
2 tablespoons lime or lemon juice
1 clove garlic, peeled and minced
1–3 *chiles chipotles en adobo*, seeded (see Glossary)
1 cup thick cream or *crème fraiche*
½ cup mixed grated Parmesan and Gruyère cheeses

Put the meat into a heavy flameproof casserole into which it fits nicely. Rub in salt, pepper, herbs, lime or lemon juice and garlic and leave to marinate for a few hours (the longer the better).

Add enough water barely to cover the meat, bring to the boil and cook steadily, uncovered, until all the liquid has evaporated and the meat starts to fry in its own rendered fat (about 40 minutes). Add a little lard only if necessary to help it brown, and turn the meat once or twice to brown evenly.

Preheat the oven to moderate (180 c, 350 f, gas 4).

Remove the pork to a board and let cool slightly to allow the juices to creep back inside, then slice neatly and fairly thickly. Set aside.

Blend together the chillies (they're EXTREMELY hot, but wonderful), cream, and salt to taste.

Arrange the slices of pork in an ovenproof dish and pour over the chilli sauce. Sprinkle on the cheese. (Can be done up to this point and set aside.) Bake for 30 minutes until bubbly and the cheese has melted. Serve with *arroz blanco con elote* (white rice with corn – see page 144) and freshly cooked spinach.

Chiles en nogada

PEPPERS STUFFED WITH MEAT, FRUIT AND ALMONDS
WITH CREAMY WALNUT SAUCE

Illustrated on front cover

This dish was created for St Augustine's Day (August 28th) by the people of Puebla to honour the self-styled Emperor Agustín de Iturbide, who'd just knocked spots off the Spaniards: always a popular move in Mexico. It is, for me, one of the glories of Mexican food at its finest: the savoury-sweet crunchy filling contrasts most happily with the soft flesh of the peppers, and the subtle creamy walnut sauce is hard to beat. It has the added advantage of looking as good as it tastes. The walnuts must be the new season's crop, otherwise they are impossible to peel.

METRIC/IMPERIAL	AMERICAN
6 large or 12 small even-sized green peppers (about 1 kg/2 lb)	6 large or 12 small equal-sized sweet green peppers (about 2 lb)
1 tablespoon lard or oil	1 tablespoon lard or oil
625 g/1¼ lb mixed minced pork and beef	1¼ lb mixed ground pork and beef
1 onion, peeled and finely chopped	1 onion, peeled and finely chopped
2 cloves garlic, peeled and crushed	2 cloves garlic, peeled and minced
2–3 fresh green chillies, seeded and finely chopped	2 fresh green chilies, seeded and finely chopped
2 large tomatoes (about 350 g/12 oz), peeled and chopped	2 large tomatoes (about ¾ lb), peeled and chopped
3 cloves	3 cloves
pinch of cumin seed	pinch of cumin seed
1-cm/½-in piece cinnamon stick	½ inch piece cinnamon stick
few black peppercorns	few black peppercorns
3 tablespoons sultanas	3 tablespoons raisins
2 tablespoons chopped almonds	2 tablespoons chopped almonds
2 tablespoons chopped candied peel	2 tablespoons chopped candied peel
1 peach or pear, stoned or cored and chopped	1 peach or pear, pitted or cored and chopped
1 apple, cored and chopped	1 apple, cored and chopped
1 banana, peeled and chopped	1 banana, peeled and chopped
salt	salt
pomegranate seeds	pomegranate seeds
parsley sprigs	parsley sprigs
SAUCE:	SAUCE:
24 fresh ('green') walnuts, shelled (about 125 g/4 oz shelled weight)	24 fresh ('green') walnuts, shelled (about ¼ lb shelled weight)
1 thick slice white bread, crusts removed	1 thick slice white bread, crusts removed
250 ml/8 fl oz milk	1 cup milk
175 ml/6 fl oz double cream or *crème fraiche*	¾ cup thick cream or *crème fraiche*
125 g/4 oz cream cheese	¼ lb cream cheese
salt	salt

Following the detailed instructions in the recipe for *chiles rellenos de queso* (see page 54), grill [broil] and peel the peppers. Remove the seed core carefully, leaving stalks intact.

Heat the lard or oil in a frying pan until very hot, then throw in the meat and fry, tossing and turning, until brown and crusty. Remove with a slotted spoon. In the same fat, fry the onion, garlic and chillies until soft but not brown. Add the tomatoes and cook until the juice evaporates. Crash the cloves, cumin, cinnamon and peppercorns about a bit in a pestle and mortar to extract the maximum flavour, then add to the chilli mixture. Return the meat to the pan. Add the raisins, almonds, peel, fruits and salt to taste, stirring to mix well. Remove from the heat and cool a little, then use to fill the peppers.

Arrange on a large round dish, and if to be served warm, cover loosely with foil and place in a warm oven. (Can be done in advance and reheated.)

To make the sauce, cover the walnuts with boiling water, then peel off the papery husk. Keep the nuts in a bowl of cold water as they are peeled to prevent discolouring. Drain the nuts and blend together with the remaining sauce ingredients in a food processor or blender to make a perfectly smooth, milky-white sauce.

To serve, pour the cold sauce over the warm stuffed peppers, sprinkle the pomegranate seeds over and garnish with lots of parsley sprigs. Alternatively, serve as a cold dish.

Chorizo

HOME MADE SPICY SAUSAGE CAKES

Illustrated on page 92

Here's a recipe for making your own chorizo in case you can't buy it easily.

METRIC/IMPERIAL	AMERICAN
500 g/1 lb boned pork, part fat/part lean	1 lb boneless pork, part fat/part lean
150 g/5 oz pork fat	5 oz fresh pork fatback
2 teaspoons chilli powder	2 teaspoons chili powder
2 tablespoons paprika	2 tablespoons paprika
generous pinch each of ground cinnamon, ground ginger, whole cloves, coriander seeds, black peppercorns, dried oregano and grated nutmeg, all ground up together	$\frac{1}{8}$ teaspoon each of ground cinnamon, ground ginger, whole cloves, coriander seeds, black peppercorns, dried oregano and grated nutmeg, all ground up together
1 large clove garlic, peeled and crushed	1 large clove garlic, peeled and minced
75 ml/3 fl oz white vinegar	6 tablespoons white vinegar
1 teaspoon salt	1 teaspoon salt

Mince [grind] the meat and the fat fairly finely in a food processor or mincer [grinder], if you can't persuade your butcher to do it for you. Then add the rest of the ingredients and, changing to the plastic blade of the food processor, process once more to blend and lighten the mixture.

Fry a little to check the seasoning, then put in a glass or enamelled bowl and leave in the refrigerator, covered with plastic wrap, to mature for at least 4–5 days.

If you're a glutton for punishment, fill the mixture into sausage casings. But since most Mexican recipes direct that you skin the chorizos, then crumble and fry them, it seems a bit of a waste of time. It is more convenient to roll them up into sausage shapes (using wet hands) and then either refrigerate or freeze. *Makes about 750 g/1 lb 10 oz chorizos, which you can form into six sausage shapes, each weighing 125 g/4 oz.*

Manchamantel

THE TABLECLOTH STAINER:

CHICKEN AND PORK IN A RED CHILLI SAUCE WITH ALMONDS AND FRUIT

METRIC/IMPERIAL

500 g/1 lb boneless stewing pork (a mixture of fat and lean, e.g. spare rib, rump, or blade bone)
1 large roasting chicken, cut in pieces, or 4–6 chicken legs
1 onion, peeled
1 carrot, peeled
1 clove garlic, peeled
1 bouquet garni (parsley, thyme, bay leaf)

SAUCE:

5 *chiles anchos*, seeded, or 4 tablespoons chilli powder
50 g/2 oz blanched almonds, or unsalted, peeled peanuts
1–2 tablespoons lard or oil
2-cm/¾-inch piece cinnamon stick, crumbled
2 cloves
6 black peppercorns
2 slices homemade-type white bread
2 large tomatoes (about 350 g/12 oz), peeled, seeded and chopped, or 1 400-g/14-oz can peeled tomatoes
2 cloves garlic, peeled
1 large onion, peeled and quartered
pinch of salt
pinch of sugar
1 tablespoon vinegar or lime juice
2 tart apples, peeled, cored and chopped
1 banana, not peeled, cut in slices
2 slices fresh pineapple, cut in triangles

AMERICAN

1 lb pork for stew (a mixture of fat and lean, e.g. boneless pork butt or Boston roast)
1 large roaster chicken, cut into pieces, or 4–6 chicken legs
1 onion, peeled
1 carrot, peeled
1 clove garlic, peeled
1 bouquet garni (parsley, thyme, bay leaf)

SAUCE:

5 *chiles anchos*, seeded, or ¼ cup chili powder
½ cup blanched almonds, or unsalted, peeled peanuts
1–2 tablespoons lard or oil
¾ inch piece cinnamon stick, crumbled
2 cloves
6 black peppercorns
2 slices homemade-type white bread
2 large tomatoes (about ¾ lb), peeled, seeded and chopped, or 1 16-oz can peeled tomatoes
2 cloves garlic, peeled
1 large onion, peeled and quartered
pinch of salt
pinch of sugar
1 tablespoon vinegar or lime juice
2 tart apples, peeled, cored and chopped
1 banana, not peeled, cut into slices
2 slices fresh pineapple, cut into triangles

Cover the pork and chicken pieces with water and simmer gently with the onion, carrot, garlic and bouquet garni until tender (about 45 minutes).

Meanwhile, make the sauce. If using whole *chiles anchos* toast them briefly (about 2–3 minutes on each side) on a griddle or in a heavy, ungreased frying pan over medium heat, squashing down and turning once. Take care not to burn the chillies or the sauce will be bitter. Remove to a bowl, cover with hot water and soak 30 minutes.

Fry the almonds or peanuts in the hot lard or oil together with the cinnamon, cloves and peppercorns until nicely toasted. Remove with a slotted spoon to a blender or food processor. Fry the bread in the same fat, and remove also to the blender or processor. When the soaking time is up, drain the chillies and add them (or the alternative chilli powder) to the blender along with the tomatoes, garlic and onion. Blend the whole business together until perfectly smooth. Add only enough stock from the meat to release the blades.

Using the same pan, reheat the oil or lard to almost smoking (add more if needed) and fry the puréed sauce, stirring all over the bottom of the pan, until well-reduced and thick. Season to taste with salt, sugar and vinegar or lime juice. Dilute to a coating consistency with more of the meat stock. Add the drained pork and chicken and prepared fruit and simmer together for a further 15 minutes or so, just enough to cook the fruit. Serve with either *arroz blanco* (white rice – see page 143) or any of the corn accompaniments to mop up the sauce, plus some plainly cooked courgettes [zucchini] or chard to give a lovely contrast of colour. *Serves 8–10.*

Carne de puerco con piña

SPICY RED PORK STEW WITH RED CHILLIES AND FRESH PINEAPPLE

Illustrated on page 89

METRIC/IMPERIAL
750 g–1 kg/1½–2 lb boneless stewing pork, cut in large cubes
salt and pepper
black peppercorns
1-cm/½-inch piece cinnamon stick
2 cloves
2 onions, peeled and chopped
1 clove garlic, peeled and crushed
2 dried red chillies, seeded and crumbled
3 large tomatoes (about 500 g/1 lb), peeled and chopped
4 thick slices fresh pineapple (about 400 g/14 oz), cut in chunks
stock as needed

AMERICAN
1½–2 lb pork for stew, cut in large cubes
salt and pepper
black peppercorns
½ inch piece cinnamon stick
2 cloves
2 onions, peeled and chopped
1 clove garlic, peeled and crushed
2 dried red chillies, seeded and crumbled
3 large tomatoes (about 1 lb), peeled and chopped
4 thick slices fresh pineapple (about 14 oz), cut into chunks
stock as needed

Put the pork in a wide heavy flameproof casserole, barely cover with water and add salt and peppercorns to taste. Cook steadily, uncovered, until the water has evaporated and the meat starts to fry in its own rendered fat. (This should take 30–40 minutes). Add a little lard if necessary to help the process. Remove the meat.

In the same fat, fry the cinnamon and cloves, then set aside. Fry the onions and garlic till golden. Add the chillies and cook, stirring, for a couple of minutes more. Throw in the tomatoes, fried spices, and salt and pepper to taste, and cook, covered, until the juices have rendered. Raise the heat and cook uncovered until the mixture is nice and thick. Stir in the pineapple chunks and check the seasoning. Add the meat and just enough stock to come half-way up the meat. Cover and cook on top of the stove or in a preheated moderate oven (180 c, 350 f, gas 4) for a further 20–30 minutes to blend the flavours. Serve with *arroz con caldo de frijól* (rice with black bean stock – see page 146) or *arroz blanco* (white rice – see page 143) and a fresh green vegetable such as courgettes [zucchini], broccoli or green beans.

Carne de puerco en chile verde

PORK IN A CREAMY PEPPER SAUCE

It is particularly important that the meat for this dish is marbled with fat, otherwise the method of cooking suggested will make it dry. If you can't get such a cut, or prefer something leaner, it would be better to start off by browning the meat, then cooking with a little wine or stock before proceeding with the frying of the sauce and the final simmer.

METRIC/IMPERIAL	AMERICAN
750 g–1 kg/1½–2 lb boned roast of pork	1½–2 lb boneless pork roast
salt and pepper	salt and pepper
2 cloves garlic	2 cloves garlic
2 green peppers	2 sweet green peppers
2 fresh green chillies	2 fresh green chilies
1 onion, peeled	1 onion, peeled
120 ml/4 fl oz double cream or *crème fraiche*	½ cup thick cream or *crème fraiche*
2 tablespoons chopped fresh coriander	2 tablespoons chopped fresh coriander
fresh coriander sprigs	fresh coriander sprigs
wafer-thin onion rings	wafer-thin onion rings

Barely cover the meat with water, add salt and pepper to taste and cook over steady heat until the water evaporates and the meat starts to fry in its own rendered fat.

While the meat is doing its thing, grill [broil] the garlic, peppers, chillies and onion until blistered and soft. Peel the garlic; quarter the onion; peel the peppers; and remove seeds and stalks from the peppers and chillies. Blend all together with the cream, chopped coriander and salt to taste in a food processor or blender until quite smooth.

When the meat has finished browning in its own fat, remove it and set aside. Fry the puréed sauce in the remaining fat until well reduced and thick. Slice the meat and give it a final simmer in the sauce to exchange flavours (about 20 minutes). Garnish with coriander sprigs and onion rings, and serve with *tamales de calabacita con flor* (cornmeal 'dumplings' with diced courgettes [zucchini] – see page 137) or a *torta de elote* (baked corn pie – see page 138) and a green vegetable.

Carnitas

CRUSTY-FRIED PORK PIECES

The name of this dish means literally 'little meaty pieces', and it is an extremely tasty and effective way to cook this rather fatty cut of pork, since nearly all the fat is rendered out in the cooking. It's the best sort of finger food, and often forms part of a large buffet spread in Mexican restaurants. *Carnitas* can also be used as a filling for *tacos* (see page 74).

METRIC/IMPERIAL	AMERICAN
2 kg/4 lb pork spare ribs (weight with bone), or about 1.5 kg/3 lb boneless belly pork, sliced	4 lb country-style spareribs (weight with bone), or about 3 lb boneless fresh pork sides, sliced
salt and pepper	salt and pepper

Using two large, wide, heavy flameproof casseroles, barely cover the pork with water and season with salt and pepper. Cook uncovered over lively heat for 30–40 minutes or until all the water has evaporated and the meat is frying in its own rendered fat. Be careful at the end: it's very easy for the meat to 'catch' and the fat to burn, so lower the heat if necessary once the water has gone and turn the pieces over and over so they brown evenly, removing them as they are ready to give the top ones a chance.

Remove to a large serving dish lined with paper towels to pick up any excess fat. Eat with the fingers, with plenty of *guacamole* or *salsa mexicana* and *frijoles veracruzanos* (black beans – see page 141) to accompany.

Lomo con chiles cuaresmeños rojos

PORK LOIN WITH FRESH RED CHILLIES

METRIC/IMPERIAL	AMERICAN
1 clove garlic, peeled and slivered	1 clove garlic, peeled and slivered
750 g–1 kg/1½–2 lb boned loin of pork	1½–2 lb boneless pork loin roast
salt and pepper	salt and pepper
juice of ½ lemon or 1 lime	juice of ½ lemon or 1 lime
2 large tomatoes (about 350 g/12 oz)	2 large tomatoes (about ¾ lb)
2 fresh red chillies	2 fresh red chilies
1 onion, peeled	1 onion, peeled
120 ml/4 fl oz double cream or *crème fraiche*	½ cup thick cream or *crème fraiche*
1–2 tablespoons lard or oil	1–2 tablespoons lard or oil
about 250 ml/8 fl oz stock	about 1 cup stock
chopped fresh coriander or *epazote*	chopped fresh coriander or *epazote*

Insert slivers of garlic at strategic intervals in the meat. Rub in salt, pepper and lemon or lime juice and leave aside to marinate.

Preheat the oven to moderate (180 C, 350 F, gas 4).

Grill [broil] the tomatoes, chillies and onion until blistered and soft. Quarter the tomatoes and onion; remove seeds and stalk from the chillies. Blend with the cream and salt to taste in a food processor or blender till smooth.

Brown the pork all over in the hot lard or oil and remove. In the same pan, fry the puréed sauce, stirring all around and scraping in all the crusty bits from frying the pork. Dilute to a coating consistency with the stock. Replace the pork in the pan, cover tightly and bake for 1–1½ hours or until a meat thermometer reads 71 C/160 F.

Slice the meat fairly thickly and place on a warm serving dish. Boil up the sauce, check seasoning and pour over the meat. Sprinkle on the chosen herbs and serve with *papas con rajas* (sauté potatoes with green chilli – see page 147) and green beans.

BEEF, LAMB AND TONGUE

The best Mexican beef comes from the northern states such as Chihuahua, Nuevo León, Sonora and Sinaloa and can of course be found in dishes all over Mexico, but never to the same extent and with the same endless variety of sauces as you find for pork or chicken.

Lamb in Mexico is really mutton, and lends itself to strong sauces and gentle steamings wrapped in leaves. It follows, therefore, that your best spring lamb is probably better off roasted in your usual way (i.e. pink in the middle and without mint and vinegar). Use these recipes for good, honest, everyday chops or as a way to cheer up one of those legs which have been languishing for ages in the freezer.

Tongue in Mexico is extremely highly prized and its smooth, tender, slightly gelatinous quality makes it an excellent foil for a hot spicy sauce. Elsewhere it tends to be relegated to the ranks of sliced, cold luncheon meat, and a really good dish of hot sliced tongue in a carefully made sauce is seldom seen.

Chiles rellenos de picadillo	Peppers stuffed with minced meat, fruit and nuts, in tomato sauce
Chuletas de carnero en salsa de almendra roja	Lamb chops with almond sauce
Albóndigas	Meatballs in tomato sauce
Carne asada a la tampiqueña	Fried beef with all the trimmings
Asado de pierna de carnero	Braised leg of lamb with tomato sauce
Estofado de carnero	Lamb stew with sultanas [raisins] and almonds
Lengua almendrada	Tongue in an almond sauce
Lengua enjitomatada	Tongue with tomatoes, chillies, sesame seeds and fruit
Tinga de lengua	Tongue with chorizo and tomatoes

Chiles rellenos de picadillo

PEPPERS STUFFED WITH MEAT

METRIC/IMPERIAL	AMERICAN
6 large, even-sized green peppers	6 large, equal-sized sweet green peppers
350 g/12 oz minced beef	$\frac{3}{4}$ lb ground beef
350 g/12 oz minced pork	$\frac{3}{4}$ lb ground pork
1 onion, peeled and chopped	1 onion, peeled and chopped
2 cloves garlic, peeled and crushed	2 cloves garlic, peeled and minced
2 fresh green chillies, seeded and chopped	2 fresh green chillies, seeded and chopped
2 large tomatoes (about 350 g/12 oz), peeled and chopped	2 large tomatoes (about $\frac{3}{4}$ lb), peeled and chopped
salt and pepper	salt and pepper
pinch each of ground cloves, cinnamon and pepper	pinch each of ground cloves, cinnamon and pepper
25 g/1 oz chopped almonds	$\frac{1}{4}$ cup chopped almonds
25 g/1 oz pine nuts or raw unsalted peanuts	$\frac{1}{4}$ cup pine nuts or raw, unsalted peanuts
25 g/1 oz sultanas	3 tablespoons golden raisins
25 g/1 oz chopped candied peel	3 tablespoons chopped candied peel
2 teaspoons vinegar	2 teaspoons vinegar
1 quantity *caldillo de jitomate* (see page 36)	1 quantity *caldillo de jitomate* (see page 36)
oil for frying	oil for frying
3 eggs, separated	3 eggs, separated
flour	flour

Following the detailed instructions in the recipe for *chiles rellenos de queso* (see page 54), grill [broil] and peel the peppers. Leaving the stalks on, make a slit down one side and very carefully ease out the seeds. Set the peppers aside.

Dry fry the meats in a heavy frying pan until the fat is rendered and the meat begins to brown. Remove with a slotted spoon. Fry the onion, garlic and chillies in the fat until soft. Add the tomatoes, and salt and pepper to taste, cover and cook till the juices run. Raise the heat and cook uncovered until somewhat reduced. Stir the meat back in and add the spices, nuts, fruit and vinegar. Cook gently for a further 10–15 minutes to blend the flavours, stirring from time to time. It should be a thick mixture. Cool slightly, then fill the prepared peppers. Close them up with a wooden toothpick, overlapping the seams a bit, and set aside.

Make up the tomato sauce in the usual way, adding a pinch of cinnamon, and being sure to use a flameproof casserole in which all six peppers will fit.

Heat oil in a large frying pan to a depth of about 1 cm/$\frac{1}{2}$ inch. Beat the egg whites to a firm snow with a pinch of salt, then briefly beat in the yolks. Dust the prepared peppers in seasoned flour, then dip them into the egg batter, twirling them about by the stem, till evenly coated. Drop them immediately into the hot oil. Fry on all sides, propping them up one against another and patching any gaps with spare batter. Remove as they are ready, drain on paper towels and place them in the simmering tomato sauce.

Serve rather soon (or they lose their crispiness) accompanied by *arroz blanco con elote* (white rice with corn – see page 144), pressed into a ring mould. (You can put the peppers with some of their sauce in the hole in the middle and serve the rest of the sauce separately.)

Chuletas de carnero en salsa de almendra roja

LAMB CHOPS IN ALMOND SAUCE

METRIC/IMPERIAL	AMERICAN
6 large or 12 small lamb chops (about 1–1.25 kg/2–2½ lb)	6 large or 12 small lamb chops (about 2–2½ lb)
salt	salt
SAUCE:	SAUCE:
1 slice French bread, cut into cubes	1 slice French bread, cut into cubes
75 g/3 oz blanched almonds	¾ cup blanched almonds
1 onion, peeled and chopped	1 onion, peeled and chopped
1 clove garlic, peeled and crushed	1 clove garlic, peeled and minced
2 small dried red chillies, crumbled	2 small dried red chilies, crumbled
dried oregano	dried oregano
1 large tomato (about 150 g/5 oz), peeled and chopped	1 large tomato (about 5 oz), peeled and chopped
350 ml/12 fl oz lamb or chicken stock	1½ cups lamb or chicken stock

Using a large shallow saucepan, barely cover the chops with water, add salt to taste and cook uncovered over steady heat until the water evaporates and the chops begin to fry in their own fat. If necessary add a little oil or lard to help them brown well, and turn once. Remove and keep warm.

In the fat remaining, fry the bread cubes, then remove them to a food processor or blender. Fry the almonds until golden; add to the processor. Fry the onion, garlic and chillies until soft but not browned. Add to the processor with the tomato and oregano and blend all together, adding only enough stock at this stage to release the blades if they're struggling a bit.

Fry the paste in the same pan as before, stirring and scraping up all the crusty bits. Dilute to a light coating consistency with the remaining stock. Place the chops in the sauce for a brief communal simmer (about 15–20 minutes).

Serve with new potatoes and *calabacitas rancheras* (courgettes [zucchini] with chillies – see page 153).

Right *carne de puerco michoacana* (page 97), served with *frijoles refritos* (page 140)
Overleaf clockwise, from the back: *arroz a la mexicana* (page 144), served in a ring mould with green beans; *albóndigas* (page 113); *estofado de carnero* (page 115)

Albóndigas

MEATBALLS IN TOMATO SAUCE

Illustrated on pages 110–111

It's a pity to call these meatballs, since the name conjures up all sorts of horrors from nursery days. Think of them rather as meat *quenelles* – after all, what are *quenelles de brochet* but pikeballs? This was our maid Audelia's recipe, and whether the idea of the cheese nuggets in the middle (instead of the hard-boiled egg, Scotch-egg-style) was her own invention, or whether it is typical of Oaxaca, her 'land', I always forgot to ask. It's a delicious touch anyway.

METRIC/IMPERIAL	AMERICAN
1 small onion, peeled	1 small onion, peeled
1 medium courgette (about 125 g/4 oz)	1 medium-size zucchini (about ¼ lb)
350 g/12 oz minced beef	¾ lb ground beef
250 g/8 oz minced pork	½ lb ground pork
1 slice stale bread, soaked in milk	1 slice stale bread, soaked in milk
pinch each of dried thyme, crumbled bay leaf, dried marjoram and ground cumin	pinch each of dried thyme, crumbled bay leaf, dried marjoram and ground cumin
2 eggs	2 eggs
salt	salt
2 quantities *caldillo de jitomate*, i.e. about 1 litre/1¾ pints sauce (see page 36)	2 quantities *caldillo de jitomate*, i.e. about 4¼ cups sauce (see page 36)
about 125 g/4 oz mature Cheddar cheese, cut in little cubes	about ¼ lb sharp Cheddar cheese, cut into little cubes

If using a food processor, chop the onion and courgette [zucchini] very finely and set aside. Change over to the plastic blade and return the onion and courgette [zucchini] to the processor. Add the meat, squeezed-out bread, herbs and spices, eggs and salt to taste. Blend really well together: the more you process or beat the mixture, the lighter will be your meatballs.

Make up the tomato sauce in the usual way, using a wide flameproof casserole. Form the meat mixture into 24 golf balls. Push a little cube of cheese into each one, closing the meat mixture around the cheese. Drop them as they are ready into the simmering sauce and cook for 25–30 minutes, by which time they should be gently swollen, with a tiny pool of melted cheese in the middle. Serve with *arroz blanco* (white rice – see page 143) and green beans.

VARIATION

For *albóndigas con chipotle* (meatballs in tomato sauce with smoked chilli flavouring), proceed as above but substitute 2–3 seeded *chiles chipotles en adobo* (see Glossary) for the fresh green chillies called for in the recipe for the *caldillo de jitomate*. Be careful as they're very hot, but their smokey flavour is unique and delicious.

Left top: *papas con rajas* (page 147); bottom: *pollo en huerto* (page 123)

Carne asada a la tampiqueña

FRIED TENDER BEEF STRIPS WITH VARIOUS GARNISHES

This is THE typical tourist dish in hotels and restaurants all over Mexico. As so often is the case with 'tourist' dishes, it can be rather disappointing, but if you do your own it's sure to be good, and it's always a hit. For up to 6 people, chat up your butcher for very thin individual strips of steak; for a party, however, I would do a tender roast of beef, marinated in a little oil and lime juice and spit-roasted, then sliced very thinly and served with the same trimmings. For each person you need:

METRIC/IMPERIAL
2 thin strips tender rump steak (tastier by far than fillet), about 18 × 6 cm and 5 mm thick/7 × 2½ inches and ¼ inch thick
salt and pepper
lime juice
oil for frying
2 *enchiladas de mole* (see page 62)
2 tablespoons *frijoles refritos* (see page 140)
lashings of *guacamole* (see page 34)
strips of pickled *chiles jalapeños*

AMERICAN
2 thin strips tender sirloin steak, about 7 × 2½ inches and ¼ inch thick
salt and pepper
lime juice
oil for frying
2 *enchiladas de mole* (see page 62)
2 tablespoons *frijoles refritos* (see page 140)
lashings of *guacamole* (see page 34)
strips of pickled *chiles jalapeños*

Beat out the steaks thinly, as if preparing veal escalopes [cutlets]. Season with salt, pepper and lime juice and let them rest a bit. Take a very heavy frying pan or griddle, give it the barest smidget of oil and heat it ferociously. Pat the steak strips dry, then sear very briefly on each side. Put straight on to a warmed plate with the *enchiladas* (tortillas dunked in *mole* sauce) and *frijoles* (puréed, fried beans) and serve the *guacamole* and chilli strips in bowls on the table.

Asado de pierna de carnero

BRAISED LEG OF LAMB IN TOMATO SAUCE

Definitely a post-conquest recipe this one, with the almonds and sherry creeping in. Very nice for a change, and a good deal more practical than the usual roast, as there's no last-minute gravy-making.

METRIC/IMPERIAL
1 small leg of lamb (about 1.5 kg/3 lb)
2 cloves garlic, peeled and slivered
25 g/1 oz blanched almonds, slivered
2–3 slices smoked streaky bacon, cut in small pieces
pinch each of ground cloves, cinnamon, salt and black pepper, all ground up together
120 ml/4 fl oz medium dry sherry
1 tablespoon lard or oil
3 large tomatoes (about 500 g/1 lb), peeled and chopped
stock or water

AMERICAN
1 small leg of lamb (about 3 lb)
2 cloves garlic, peeled and slivered
¼ cup slivered blanched almonds
2–3 slices bacon, cut into small pieces
pinch each of ground cloves, cinnamon, salt and pepper, all ground up together
½ cup medium dry sherry
1 tablespoon lard or oil
3 large tomatoes (about 1 lb), peeled and chopped
stock or water

Make cuts all over the leg of lamb and insert slivers of garlic, almonds and bacon pieces. Rub in the spices, pour over the sherry and leave overnight.

Dry the meat, reserving the marinade, and brown in hot lard or oil in a flameproof casserole. Remove and in the same fat fry the tomatoes, stirring until thick. Add the reserved marinade, check seasoning and replace the lamb. Add stock or water to come two-thirds of the way up the meat, cover with foil and a lid and either simmer on top of the stove, or bake in a preheated moderate oven (180 c, 350 f, gas 4), for 1–1½ hours or until tender. Do not let it do more than a very gentle simmer or it will be dry and lifeless.

Remove the meat to a serving dish, carve in neat but thickish slices and keep warm. Boil down the juices if necessary to thicken and reduce, and pour over the meat. Serve with *acelgas con crema* (chard with spicy cream sauce – see page 156) and *tortitas de papa* (potato pancakes – see page 147).

Estofado de carnero

LAMB STEW WITH CHILLIES, SULTANAS [RAISINS] AND TOMATOES

Illustrated on pages 110–111

METRIC/IMPERIAL	AMERICAN
1 kg/2 lb boned lamb shoulder, cut in chunks	2 lb boneless lamb shoulder, cut into chunks
salt and pepper	salt and pepper
2–3 small dried red chillies, crumbled, or 1 tablespoon cayenne pepper	2–3 small dried red chilies, crumbled, or 1 tablespoon cayenne
1 onion, peeled and chopped	1 onion, peeled and chopped
2 cloves garlic, peeled and crushed	2 cloves garlic, peeled and minced
pinch each of ground cinnamon, cloves, salt and pepper, all ground up together	pinch each of ground cinnamon, cloves, salt and pepper, all ground up together
25 g/1 oz blanched almonds	¼ cup blanched almonds
25 g/1 oz sultanas	3 tablespoons golden raisins
3 large tomatoes (about 500 g/1 lb), or 1 400-g/14-oz can tomatoes	3 large tomatoes (about 1 lb), or 1 16-oz can tomatoes
250 ml/8 fl oz stock	1 cup stock
125 ml/4 fl oz dry sherry	½ cup dry sherry
1 tablespoon vinegar	1 tablespoon vinegar
1 bay leaf	1 bay leaf

Barely cover the meat cubes with water and add salt and pepper to taste. Cook uncovered over moderate heat until the liquid has evaporated and the meat is frying in its own rendered fat. Lower the heat towards the end so the meat doesn't burn. Remove when it is a nice golden brown. In the same fat fry the chillies or cayenne, onion, garlic, spices, almonds and sultanas [raisins] until the almonds are golden and the sultanas [raisins] plump. Add the tomatoes and cook until thick. Moisten with the stock, sherry and vinegar.

Replace the meat, add the bay leaf, cover with foil and a lid and cook for a further 20–30 minutes on top of the stove, or in a preheated moderate oven (180 c, 350 f, gas 4), until quite tender and the flavours nicely blended. It should be just pleasantly spicy, not too hot. Serve with *chayotes rellenos* (stuffed chow chow or kohlrabi – see page 156) and a *corona de arroz* (white or red rice baked in a ring mould – see pages 143 and 144).

Lengua almendrada

TONGUE IN AN ALMOND SAUCE WITH GREEN OLIVES AND CHILLIES

Illustrated on pages 90–91

This is an unusual dish and fine for a dinner party: the firm, smooth texture of the tongue contrasts pleasingly with the nutty sauce, and optional 'heat' can be added at the table for those who don't feel Mexican food is quite right without a bit of bite.

METRIC/IMPERIAL	AMERICAN
1 ox tongue	1 ox tongue
1 clove garlic, peeled	1 clove garlic, peeled
1 onion, peeled	1 onion, peeled
1 carrot, peeled	1 carrot, peeled
1 bouquet garni (thyme, parsley, bay leaf)	1 bouquet garni (thyme, parsley, bay leaf)
salt	salt
12 green olives	12 green olives
2 canned green chillies, drained and cut in strips	2 canned green chilies, drained and cut into strips
SAUCE:	SAUCE:
2 large tomatoes (about 350 g/12 oz)	2 large tomatoes (about $\frac{3}{4}$ lb)
1 clove garlic	1 clove garlic
1 small onion, peeled	1 small onion, peeled
1 tablespoon lard or oil	1 tablespoon lard or oil
2 thick slices French bread, cubed	2 thick slices French bread, cubed
50 g/2 oz unblanched almonds	$\frac{1}{2}$ cup unblanched almonds
2 cloves	2 cloves
6 black peppercorns	6 black peppercorns
1-cm/$\frac{1}{2}$-inch piece cinnamon stick	$\frac{1}{2}$ inch piece cinnamon stick
salt	salt
250 ml/8 fl oz medium sherry or white wine	1 cup medium sherry or white wine

Cook the tongue in water to cover with the garlic, onion, carrot, bouquet garni, and salt to taste for about 2 hours or until a skewer meets minimal opposition when stuck into the thickest part of the tongue. Let the tongue cool in the stock, then drain, reserving the stock. Skin the tongue.

Grill [broil] the tomatoes, garlic and onion until blistered and soft. Quarter the tomatoes and onion; peel the garlic. Place all in a blender or food processor.

Heat the lard or oil and fry the bread cubes and almonds, tossing and turning, till golden. Remove with a slotted spoon to the blender or food processor and blend with the tomatoes, garlic and onion. Add the cloves, peppercorns, cinnamon, and salt to taste and blend till really smooth.

Using the same pan (which had better be a deep one, or the mess will be indescribable), reheat the lard or oil and throw in the purée. Clamp on the splatter shield or lid and cook for 5–10 minutes, stirring from time to time, until well seasoned and thick. Dilute to a coating consistency with some of the reserved tongue stock and the sherry or wine.

Cut the tongue into 1 cm/$\frac{1}{2}$ inch thick slices and place in the sauce. Simmer for a further 25–30 minutes.

To serve, place on a long, beautiful serving dish and scatter on the olives and chilli strips (or serve them at the table if you prefer: the canned *chiles jalapeños* are EXTREMELY hot). Serve with *arroz blanco con elote* (white rice with corn kernels – see page 144) or a *torta de elote* (corn torte – see page 138) and *acelgas con crema* (chard with chillies and cream – see page 156).

Lengua enjitomatada

TONGUE WITH TOMATOES, SESAME SEEDS, BANANAS AND
SULTANAS [RAISINS]

METRIC/IMPERIAL	AMERICAN
1 ox tongue	1 beef tongue
1 onion, peeled	1 onion, peeled
1 clove garlic, peeled	1 clove garlic, peeled
1 bouquet garni (parsley, thyme, bay leaf)	1 bouquet garni (parsley, thyme, bay leaf)
salt	salt
SAUCE:	SAUCE:
1 onion, peeled and chopped	1 onion, peeled and chopped
2 cloves garlic, peeled and crushed	2 cloves garlic, peeled and minced
1 tablespoon lard or oil	1 tablespoon lard or oil
2 large tomatoes (about 350 g/12 oz), peeled and chopped	2 large tomatoes (about $\frac{3}{4}$ lb), peeled and chopped
2–3 small dried red chillies, seeded and crumbled	2–3 small dried red chilies, seeded and crumbled
1 plantain or 2 unripe bananas, peeled and sliced	1 plantain or 2 unripe bananas, peeled and sliced
salt	salt
1 tablespoon sesame seeds	1 tablespoon sesame seeds
25 g/1 oz sultanas	3 tablespoons raisins

Cook the tongue with the onion, garlic, bouquet garni, and salt to taste in water to cover for about 2 hours. Leave to cool in the stock.

Soften the onion and garlic in the lard or oil. Add the tomatoes, chillies, plantain or bananas and salt to taste. Cover and cook until the tomato juices run, then uncover and cook, stirring from time to time, until well reduced and thick. Stir in the sesame seeds and raisins and continue cooking until the raisins plump up nicely (about 10 minutes more). Dilute to a light coating consistency with some of the tongue stock and leave to simmer gently.

Skin and slice the drained tongue fairly thickly. Marry it up with the sauce and give the final product a further 20–30 minutes cooking to blend the flavours.

Serve with plain *tamales* (steamed cornmeal parcels – see page 135) or *frijoles compuestos* (tarted-up canned beans – see page 142) and some *calabacitas rancheras* (courgettes [zucchini] with chillies and peppers – see page 153) or *calabacitas rellenas de elote* (corn-stuffed courgettes [zucchini] – see page 154), which look rather nice surrounding the meat.

Tinga de lengua

BRAISED TONGUE WITH CHORIZO SAUSAGE AND TOMATOES

The *tingas* from Puebla are a series of savoury stews whose most distinguishing ingredients are chorizo and the delicious, smoked *chile chipotle*, plus one or two other goodies. There are many versions, some using pork some using chicken, and in this case tongue. If you aren't yet quite converted to the idea of tongue, you could use the same sauce with a different meat.

METRIC/IMPERIAL	AMERICAN
1 ox tongue (fresh or smoked)	1 beef tongue (fresh or smoked)
black peppercorns	black peppercorns
1 bay leaf	1 bay leaf
1 onion, peeled	1 onion, peeled
1 clove garlic, peeled	1 clove garlic, peeled
salt	salt
1 avocado, peeled, stoned and cut in 8 segments to garnish	1 avocado, peeled, seeded and cut into 8 segments for garnish
SAUCE:	SAUCE:
2 chorizos (about 250 g/8 oz), skinned and crumbled	2 chorizos (about ½ lb), skinned and crumbled
1 onion, peeled and chopped	1 onion, peeled and chopped
1 clove garlic, peeled and crushed	1 clove garlic, peeled and minced
3 large tomatoes (about 500 g/1 lb), grilled and puréed, or 1 400-g/14-oz can tomatoes, puréed with their juice	3 large tomatoes (about 1 lb), broiled and puréed, or 1 16-oz can tomatoes, puréed with their juice
½ teaspoon black peppercorns, 2 cloves and 1-cm/½-inch piece cinnamon stick, toasted together	½ teaspoon black peppercorns, 2 cloves and ½ inch piece cinnamon stick, toasted together
2–3 canned *chiles chipotles en adobo*, drained, seeded and chopped, or 2 dried *chiles chipotles*, seeded and crumbled	2–3 canned *chiles chipotles en adobo*, drained, seeded and chopped, or 2 dried *chiles chipotles*, seeded and crumbled
salt	salt

Cook the tongue with the peppercorns, bay leaf, onion, garlic, and salt to taste in water to cover for about 2 hours, or until a skewer pierces the thickest part easily. Let it cool in its own stock.

Dry fry the chorizos in a heavy pan or flameproof casserole until the fat is rendered. Remove with a slotted spoon. In the same fat soften the onion and garlic. Raise the heat a bit and throw in the puréed tomatoes, the toasted spices, chillies and salt to taste. Fry till thick and tasty, then replace the chorizo and dilute if necessary to a light coating consistency with some of the tongue stock.

Skin and slice the drained tongue, place it in the sauce and give it all a final bubble up for about 20 minutes to blend flavours. (Or you can prepare it up to this point, leaving the final simmer until just before serving.)

Arrange on a beautiful serving dish, garnish with the avocado segments and serve with *arroz blanco* (white rice – see page 143) or *tamales blancos* (steamed cornmeal parcels – see page 136) and green beans for a nice contrast of colour.

CHICKEN, RABBIT, DUCK AND TURKEY

The chickens in Mexico (like the pork) are marvellous, full of maize and flavour and served in a never-ending variety of sauces. However, even if you can't get such choice birds, the weariest old battery hen will perk up no end if treated according to any of the suggestions that follow. Rabbit and turkey both make good, rather neutral backgrounds to strong sauces, while duck turns up in a rather unusual guise.

Pechugas con rajas	Chicken breasts with creamy pepper sauce
Pollo en nogada	Chicken in walnut and red chilli sauce
Pollo en mole verde de pepitas	Chicken in pumpkin seed and almond sauce
Pollo en huerto	Chicken casserole with fruits and vegetables
Mole de guajolote o pollo	Turkey in dark chilli sauce with nuts, fruit, seeds and chocolate
Pavo al horno	Orange-basted turkey with pork, fruit and nut stuffing
Tinga de Puebla	Chicken with tomatoes, chillies and sardines
Pato en pipián rojo de ajonjolí	Duck in red sesame seed sauce
Conejo a la criolla	Rabbit in a hazelnut and saffron sauce

Pechugas con rajas

CHICKEN OR TURKEY BREAST WITH CHILLIES

This recipe is adapted from Diana Kennedy's recipe *pechugas de pollo con rajas*. It makes a wonderful buffet dish for 8–10 if you double the quantities.

METRIC/IMPERIAL	AMERICAN
4 small fresh green chillies, or 1 113-g/4-oz can peeled green chillies, drained	4 small fresh green chilies, or 1 4-oz can peeled green chilies, drained
6–8 skinned and boned chicken breasts or turkey escalopes (about 750 g/1½ lb)	6–8 skinless, boneless chicken breasts or turkey cutlets (about 1½ lb)
salt and pepper	salt and pepper
1 teaspoon oil	1 teaspoon oil
25 g/1 oz butter	2 tablespoons butter
2 large onions, peeled and thinly sliced	2 large onions, peeled and thinly sliced
4 green peppers, grilled and peeled (see page 54)	4 sweet green peppers, broiled and peeled (see page 54)
120 ml/4 fl oz milk	½ cup milk
250 ml/8 fl oz double cream or *crème fraiche*	1 cup heavy cream or *crème fraiche*
125 g/4 oz Cheddar cheese, grated	1 cup grated Cheddar cheese

If using fresh chillies, grill [broil] them until blistered and soft. Remove seeds and stalks, and cut the chillies into fine strips. Set aside. Preheat the oven to moderate (180 c, 350 f, gas 4).

Cut the chicken or turkey into finger-size strips and dry well on paper towels. Season with salt and pepper then sauté briefly in the hot oil and butter in a large frying pan until golden. Remove with a slotted spoon to a long ovenproof serving dish and set aside.

In the same pan, cook the onions gently until soft and golden. Meanwhile, put half of the prepared peppers and chillies into a food processor or blender with the milk, cream, and ½ teaspoon salt and blend to a smooth sauce. Add the remaining peppers and chillies to the onions, and cook gently a further 5–10 minutes or until soft.

Sprinkle the pepper, onion and chilli mixture over the meat, pour on the sauce and scatter on the grated cheese. (The dish can wait at this point.) Bake for about 30 minutes or until well heated through, golden and bubbly.

Serve with *arroz blanco con elote* (white rice with corn kernels – see page 144) and *calabacitas con jitomate* (courgettes [zucchini] with tomatoes – see page 154).

Pollo en nogada

CHICKEN IN A WALNUT SAUCE WITH RED CHILLI

METRIC/IMPERIAL

6–8 chicken leg joints (i.e. thigh-with-drumstick), or 1 2-kg/4-lb chicken, cut in 6–8 serving pieces
black peppercorns
1 onion, peeled
1 clove garlic, peeled
1 bouquet garni (parsley, thyme, bay leaf)
salt

SAUCE:

4–6 *chiles anchos*, or 4 tablespoons chilli powder
1-cm/½-inch piece cinnamon stick
3 black peppercorns
2 cloves
75 g/3 oz raw unsalted peanuts
75 g/3 oz walnut halves
1 large slice bread, cubed
2 onions, peeled and quartered
2 cloves garlic, peeled and crushed
1 tablespoon lard or oil
salt

AMERICAN

6–8 chicken leg portions (i.e. thigh-with-drumstick), or 1 4-lb chicken, cut into 6–8 serving pieces
black peppercorns
1 onion, peeled
1 clove garlic, peeled
1 bouquet garni (parsley, thyme, bay leaf)
salt

SAUCE:

4–6 *chiles anchos*, or ¼ cup chili powder
½ inch piece cinnamon stick
3 black peppercorns
2 cloves
¾ cup raw unsalted peanuts
1 cup walnut halves
1 large slice bread, cubed
2 onions, peeled and quartered
2 cloves garlic, peeled and minced
1 tablespoon lard or oil
salt

Cook the chicken pieces with the peppercorns, onion, garlic, bouquet garni, and salt to taste in water to cover for 25–30 minutes. Leave to cool in the stock.

Soften the chillies (if using whole *chiles anchos*) on a griddle or heavy ungreased frying pan until supple and fragrant. Remove seeds and stalks, tear in rough pieces and soak in hot water for about 20 minutes or until floppy. Toast the cinnamon, peppercorns and cloves and set aside.

Fry the nuts, bread cubes, onion and garlic in the hot lard or oil until golden brown. Scrape into a blender or food processor and add the toasted spices, drained chillies (or chilli powder), and salt to taste. Blend till smooth, adding a little stock from the chicken to release the blades; the sauce should be smooth. (In order to get the best flavour, you need to fry the very concentrated purée first, *then* add more stock.)

Add more lard or oil to the frying pan to make 1 tablespoon, heat to almost smoking and throw in the puréed sauce. Fry hard, stirring well, until well reduced and thick. Dilute with a little more stock to give a lightly coating consistency.

Add the drained chicken pieces and simmer for a further 15–20 minutes to heat through and blend flavours. Serve with *arroz a la mexicana* (red rice – see page 144) or *tortitas de papa* (potato pancakes – see page 147) and a green vegetable.

Pollo en mole verde de pepitas

CHICKEN IN A PUMPKIN SEED AND ALMOND SAUCE

Just near the rather smart club where we used to play tennis in Cuernavaca was a distinctly un-smart place called *Mi Cabaña* (My Cabin). It was only open at weekends and on public holidays and it only served a choice of two *moles*: *verde* and *poblano*, accompanied by rice and tortillas which were patted out by hand before our eyes. The smell of drains was all-pervasive, and the simplicity of it all was disarming, but they were *moles* never to be forgotten.

METRIC/IMPERIAL

6–8 chicken leg joints (i.e. thigh-with-drumstick) or breasts, or 1 2-kg/4-lb chicken, cut in 6–8 serving pieces
black peppercorns
1 bay leaf
salt

SAUCE:

50 g/2 oz blanched almonds
125 g/4 oz green, shelled, unsalted pumpkin seeds
2 tablespoons oil or lard
6 black peppercorns
pinch of aniseed or cumin seed
1 15-oz/425-g can Mexican green tomatoes, drained, or 350 g/12 oz fresh Mexican green tomatoes, peeled, or 350 g/12 oz green gooseberries, topped and tailed, (or even 500 g/1 lb sorrel, blanched and squeezed dry)
3–4 fresh green chillies, seeded, or 2 canned *chiles jalapeños en escabeche*, drained
1 onion, peeled and quartered
2 cloves garlic, peeled
4 large lettuce leaves (e.g. cos)
salt

AMERICAN

6–8 chicken leg portions (i.e. thigh-with-drumstick), or 1 4-lb chicken, cut into 6–8 serving pieces
black peppercorns
1 bay leaf
salt

SAUCE:

½ cup blanched almonds
½ cup green, shelled, unsalted pumpkin seeds
2 tablespoons oil or lard
6 black peppercorns
pinch of aniseed or cumin seed
1 16-oz can Mexican green tomatoes, drained, or ¾ lb fresh Mexican green tomatoes (about 20), peeled, or ¾ lb green gooseberries, trimmed (or even 1 lb sorrel, blanched and squeezed dry)
3–4 fresh green chillies, seeded, or 2 canned *chiles jalapeños en escabeche*, drained
1 onion, peeled and quartered
2 cloves garlic, peeled
4 large lettuce leaves (e.g. romaine)
salt

Cover the chicken with water, add the peppercorns, bay leaf, and salt to taste and simmer until tender (about 25–30 minutes). Leave to cool in the stock.

In a large, heavy frying pan, fry the almonds and pumpkin seeds in 1 tablespoon of the oil or lard, using a splatter shield as they are apt to leap about in a rather explosively Mexican way. When evenly golden (shake them from time to time, and don't let them burn or the sauce will be bitter), remove with a slotted spoon and leave to cool. Keep the pan and any oil for later.

Grind the cooled seeds and almonds dry in a food processor or blender together with the peppercorns and aniseed or cumin. Add about 500 ml/16 fl oz [2 cups] of the stock from the chicken and blend thoroughly. (It is important first to grind the seeds and spices dry, then to add the stock, as the flavour is markedly affected.) Pour this mixture into a bowl. Place the tomatoes, gooseberries or sorrel, the chillies, onion, garlic, lettuce leaves and salt to taste in the food processor or blender and blend till smooth. Push it through a sieve or food mill, pressing down well on the debris to extract all the juice.

Heat the fat in the frying pan, adding the remaining oil or lard if necessary, then throw in the strained sauce. Fry hard, stirring well, until well-seasoned and thick. Stir in the pumpkin seed mixture, whisking well. Taste for seasoning. The sauce should be of a lightly coating consistency (dilute with more chicken stock if necessary) and have a nutty, toasted flavour with a pleasant glow from the chillies. Simmer gently for 20–30 minutes.

Put in the chicken pieces and cook for a further 15–20 minutes to flavour them well. The oil from the seeds will float to the top, but it doesn't matter: whisk it up a bit and it will come together. Serve with *arroz a la mexicana* (see page 144) and a *torta de elote* (corn torte – see page 138).

Pollo en huerto

CHICKEN WITH VEGETABLES AND FRUIT

Illustrated on page 112

You can use a *römertopf* (chicken brick) for this dish to great advantage, but the initial frying will have to be done in a pan.

METRIC/IMPERIAL	AMERICAN
6–8 chicken leg joints (i.e. thigh-with-drumstick), or 1 2-kg/4-lb chicken, cut in 6–8 serving pieces	6–8 chicken leg portions (i.e. thigh-with-drumstick), or 1 4-lb chicken, cut into 6–8 serving pieces
salt and pepper	salt and pepper
1 tablespoon oil or lard	1 tablespoon oil or lard
1 onion, peeled and sliced	1 onion, peeled and sliced
2 cloves garlic, peeled and chopped	2 cloves garlic, peeled and chopped
1 large tomato (about 150 g/5 oz), peeled and chopped	1 large tomato (about 5 oz), peeled and chopped
pinch of ground cinnamon	pinch of ground cinnamon
pinch of ground cloves	pinch of ground cloves
1 pear, cored and sliced	1 pear, cored and sliced
1 tart apple (e.g. Granny Smiths), cored and sliced	1 tart apple, cored and sliced
1 peach, stoned and sliced	1 peach, pitted and sliced
1 medium courgette (about 125 g/4 oz), cut in rounds	1 medium-size zucchini (about ¼ lb), cut into rounds
2 tablespoons fresh breadcrumbs	2 tablespoons soft bread crumbs

Preheat the oven to moderate (180 c, 350 f, gas 4). Season the chicken pieces with salt and pepper. Brown the chicken pieces all over in the hot oil or lard in a frying pan, and remove. Soften the onion and garlic in the frying pan, then add the tomato, spices, and salt and pepper to taste. Cover and cook till the juices render. Uncover, raise the heat and cook till somewhat reduced.

Layer the chicken pieces with the tomato mixture, pear, apple, peach and courgette [zucchini] in a *römertopf* (chicken brick) or large flameproof casserole, not forgetting to season as you go. Sprinkle on the breadcrumbs, cover tightly and bake for about 40 minutes or until the chicken is tender and the juices no longer run pink.

Serve the chicken in the *römertopf* or casserole with crusty *papas con rajas* (sauté potatoes with chilli and onion – see page 147), or any of the rice dishes.

Mole de guajolote o pollo

TURKEY OR CHICKEN IN A CHILLI SAUCE WITH
HERBS, SPICES, SEEDS AND NUTS

Illustrated on pages 130–131

Most Mexican housewives (or cooks) would buy their *mole* at the special spices stall in the market in the form of a very concentrated paste, to be thinned down later with a good stock and served with the turkey or chicken. They would look at you with total disbelief if you airily let drop the fact that you had made your own from scratch, and certainly you can reckon to have really passed the acid test as far as genuine Mexican cooking is concerned when you have mastered this recipe. It is a superb, festive, sumptuously rich, colourful dish, ideal for a party. Either do it for 12, as given here, or halve the quantities and do in addition the *pollo en mole verde de pepitas* (see page 122) for a *mole* party – and don't forget the *tamales*.

METRIC/IMPERIAL	AMERICAN
about 3 kg/6½ lb turkey or chicken pieces	about 6½ lb turkey or chicken pieces
1–2 tablespoons lard or oil	1–2 tablespoons lard or oil
1 carrot, peeled	1 carrot, peeled
1 onion, peeled	1 onion, peeled
1 clove garlic	1 clove garlic
black peppercorns	black peppercorns
1 bay leaf	1 bay leaf
salt	salt
2 tablespoons sesame seeds to garnish	2 tablespoons sesame seeds for garnish
SAUCE:	SAUCE:
8 *chiles anchos*	8 *chiles anchos*
4 *chiles mulatos*	4 *chiles mulatos*
2 *chiles pasilla*	2 *chiles pasilla*
6 black peppercorns	6 black peppercorns
6 coriander seeds	6 coriander seeds
2-cm/¾-inch piece cinnamon stick	¾ inch piece cinnamon stick
4 cloves	4 cloves
pinch of aniseed or fennel seeds	pinch of aniseed or fennel seeds
4 tablespoons sesame seeds	¼ cup sesame seeds
3 large tomatoes (about 500 g/1 lb)	3 large tomatoes (about 1 lb)
2 cloves garlic	2 cloves garlic
1 large onion, peeled	1 large onion, peeled
75 g/3 oz sultanas	½ cup raisins
2 tablespoons lard or oil	2 tablespoons lard or oil
125 g/4 oz unblanched almonds	1 cup unblanched almonds
2 fat slices homemade-type bread, cut into cubes	2 fat slices homemade-type bread, cut into cubes
2 stale tortillas, cut in strips	2 stale tortillas, cut into strips
75 g/3 oz green, shelled, unsalted pumpkin seeds	⅓ cup green, shelled, unsalted pumpkin seeds
2 tablespoons vinegar	2 tablespoons vinegar
25 g/1 oz plain chocolate, broken into pieces	1 oz (1 square) semi-sweet chocolate, broken into pieces
salt	salt

Dry the turkey or chicken pieces well on paper towels and brown in the hot lard or oil in a large, heavy flameproof casserole until golden all over. You will have to do this in several batches. Tip off any excess fat, then replace all the meat. Add water to cover, the carrot, onion, garlic, peppercorns, bay leaf, and salt to taste and simmer until just tender, 35–40 minutes. Leave to cool in the stock while you embark on the rest.

Toast the chillies gently on a griddle or ungreased heavy frying pan until supple and fragrant, pressing down well with the back of a palette knife or spatula. Remove the stalks, cut open and tip out the seeds and tear the chillies in rough pieces. Put to soak in hot water for at least 20 minutes or until floppy.

Toast the peppercorns, coriander seeds, cinnamon, cloves, aniseed or fennel seeds and sesame seeds on the same griddle. Set aside to cool.

Grill [broil] the tomatoes, garlic and onion until blistered and nicely toasted. Quarter the tomatoes (don't skin them) and onion. Slip the garlic out of its overcoat. Set aside.

Using a large, wide pan, fry the sultanas [raisins] until plump in 1 tablespoon of the lard or oil, then remove. Fry the almonds, bread cubes, tortilla strips and pumpkin seeds, adding more lard or oil if necessary, and tossing and stirring until evenly golden. Be careful with the pumpkin seeds: they are apt to explode all over the place in a rather Mexican fashion. Set aside to cool, with the sultanas [raisins].

Drain the chillies, then blend them in a blender or food processor until smooth with half the tomatoes, onion and garlic. Using a large, heavy flameproof casserole into which everything will eventually fit, heat a thin film of lard or oil until nearly smoking. Throw in the chilli purée and fry, stirring all over and round about until thick and well-reduced.

In the same blender jar or food processor (don't wash – it's all the same in the end), blend the remaining tomatoes, onion and garlic with the toasted seeds, spices, sultanas [raisins], almonds, bread and tortillas. Do it in two batches if you can't fit it all in (and give thanks for your blender/processor – in Mexico you'd be down on your hunkers grinding it by hand on a flat pestle and mortar . . .). It should be really smooth – add a little stock from the turkey only if necessary to release the blades. Add this mixture to the chilli purée in the casserole, mixing well, and continue to cook, stirring, until really thick and pasty. (This, in fact, is the paste you would buy in the market. This recipe can be prepared ahead up to this point.) Stir in the vinegar and chocolate pieces, plus enough turkey stock to give a light coating consistency. Season to taste with salt and simmer for a further 30 minutes.

Add the drained turkey or chicken pieces to the sauce and give the whole thing a final simmer for about 20 minutes to impregnate well with the sauce.

To serve, arrange the turkey or chicken pieces on a large serving dish. Coat with the sauce, sprinkle on the sesame seeds and serve with plain *tamales* (steamed cornmeal dumplings – see page 135). *Serves 12.*

Note: *Mole*, in common with all other Mexican sauces, improves with age, so make it at least 2 days before needed and let it ripen. It also freezes very well – to save on freezer space, you could freeze the concentrated paste, continuing later with the addition of vinegar, chocolate, stock and seasonings.

Pavo al horno

SEVILLE ORANGE-BASTED TURKEY STUFFED WITH PORK, NUTS AND
FRUIT

Turkeys are so much a part of our whole Christmas scene that it's easy to forget that they came to us from Mexico in the first place. Try this one for a change to smarten up the old bird . . .

METRIC/IMPERIAL
1 4–5-kg/9–11-lb turkey
juice of 3 Seville oranges (or 2 oranges
  and 1 lemon if you can't get Sevilles)
120 ml/4 fl oz tasteless salad oil
1 clove garlic, peeled and crushed
1 onion, peeled and chopped
salt and pepper
turkey stock made from the giblets
STUFFING:
1 onion, peeled and finely chopped
1 clove garlic, peeled and crushed
1 tablespoon lard or oil
1 large tomato (about 150 g/5 oz), peeled
  and chopped
1–2 fresh or canned green chillies, seeded
  and finely chopped
25 g/1 oz sultanas
25 g/1 oz diced candied orange or lemon
  peel
1 banana, peeled and sliced
1 tart apple, peeled, cored and chopped
50 g/2 oz blanched almonds, chopped
salt and pepper
500 g/1 lb minced pork (a mixture of fat
  and lean)
1 egg
mixed spices to taste (cloves, nutmeg and
  cinnamon)

AMERICAN
1 9–11-lb turkey
juice of 3 Seville oranges (or 2 oranges
  and 1 lemon if you can't get Sevilles)
½ cup tasteless salad oil
1 clove garlic, peeled and minced
1 onion, peeled and chopped
salt and pepper
turkey stock made from the giblets
STUFFING:
1 onion, peeled and finely chopped
1 clove garlic, peeled and minced
1 tablespoon lard or oil
1 large tomato (about 5 oz), peeled and
  chopped
1–2 fresh or canned green chilies, seeded
  and finely chopped
1 oz golden raisins
1 oz diced candied orange or lemon peel
1 banana, peeled and sliced
1 tart apple, peeled, cored and chopped
⅓ cup chopped blanched almonds
salt and pepper
1 lb ground pork (a mixture of fat and
  lean)
1 egg
mixed spices to taste (cloves, nutmeg and
  cinnamon)

Blend together the orange juice, oil, garlic, onion, and salt and pepper to taste. Set aside.

For the stuffing, soften the onion and garlic in the lard or oil without browning. Add the tomato and chillies, cover and cook until the juice runs. Uncover and raise the heat to evaporate and concentrate. Add the prepared fruits, almonds, and salt and pepper to taste, and cook, stirring, until well-mixed. Allow to cool slightly, then mix with the pork, egg and spices, beating well or processing using the plastic blade to lighten and blend. Chill well.

Stuff the turkey, sew up and truss firmly. Place in a large roasting pan and pour over the orange juice mixture. Let it marinate in a cool place overnight so the flavours can penetrate the skin.

Preheat the oven to moderate (180 c, 350 f, gas 4).

Add enough stock (or stock and white wine) to come about one-quarter of the way up the bird. Cover with a dome of foil and roast for about 2½ hours, basting regularly with the orange juices and stock. Remove the foil for the last 30 minutes so the bird will brown.

For a change (since you're obviously in the mood if you've got this far) you could serve with a *torta de elote* (baked corn torte – see page 138); but the Brussels sprouts will have to stay – better than sweets any day . . .

Tinga de Puebla

CHICKEN PIECES WITH CHILLI, AVOCADO AND SARDINES

An unlikely mixture (the word *tinga* apparently means 'a mess'), but nonetheless delicious. The *tingas* normally contain as standard the smoked *chile chipotle* and *chorizo*; sometimes, like this one, they add a touch of sardines. Don't be alarmed – it's a delicious 'mess'.

METRIC/IMPERIAL
6–8 chicken leg joints (i.e. thigh-with-drumstick) or breasts, or 1 2-kg/4-lb chicken, cut in 6–8 serving pieces
1 onion, peeled
1 clove garlic
1 bay leaf
salt
1 avocado, peeled, stoned and cut in 8 segments
SAUCE:
1 onion, peeled and chopped
1 clove garlic, peeled and crushed
1 tablespoon lard or oil
2 large tomatoes (about 350 g/12 oz), peeled and chopped
2 tablespoons chopped parsley
salt and pepper
250 g/8 oz potatoes, cooked, peeled and cubed
1 125-g/4-oz can sardines, drained and mashed
2 *chiles chipotles en vinagre*, or 2 fresh green chillies

AMERICAN
6–8 chicken leg portions (i.e. thigh-with-drumstick), or 1 4-lb chicken, cut into 6–8 serving pieces
1 onion, peeled
1 clove garlic
1 bay leaf
salt
1 avocado, peeled, seeded and cut into 8 segments
SAUCE:
1 onion, peeled and chopped
1 clove garlic, peeled and minced
1 tablespoon lard or oil
2 large tomatoes (about $\frac{3}{4}$ lb), peeled and chopped
2 tablespoons chopped parsley
salt and pepper
$\frac{1}{2}$ lb potatoes, cooked, peeled and cubed
1 4-oz can sardines, drained and mashed
2 *chiles chipotles en vinagre*, or 2 fresh green chillies

Cook the chicken pieces in water to cover with the onion, garlic, bay leaf, and salt to taste until just tender (25–30 minutes). Leave to cool in the stock.

Soften the onion and garlic in the lard or oil without browning. Add the tomatoes, parsley, and salt and pepper to taste. Cover and cook gently until the juices exude. Uncover and cook fast until somewhat reduced. Stir in the potato cubes and the mashed sardines and cook, stirring, until well mixed. Moisten with about 500 ml/16 fl oz [2 cups] of the stock from the chicken.

Add the drained chicken and chillies (whole) and simmer a final 10–15 minutes to blend flavours and for the chillies to wander through the sauce and impart a gentle glow. Garnish with the avocado segments and serve with *calabacitas rancheras* (courgettes [zucchini] with green chilli – see page 153).

Pato en pipián rojo de ajonjolí

DUCK IN RED SESAME SEED SAUCE

Illustrated on pages 130–131

Similar to the one they serve in the Hacienda de Los Morales in Mexico City (one of the few 'elegant' restaurants to include real Mexican food in their menu), this dish could equally well be done with chicken or turkey.

METRIC/IMPERIAL	AMERICAN
1 2-kg/4-lb duck, cut in serving pieces	1 4-lb duck, cut into serving pieces
salt	salt
black peppercorns	black peppercorns
1 bay leaf	1 bay leaf
1 onion, peeled	1 onion, peeled
1 clove garlic	1 clove garlic
SAUCE:	SAUCE:
4 *chiles anchos*, or 4 tablespoons chilli powder	4 *chiles anchos*, or $\frac{1}{4}$ cup chili powder
125 g/4 oz sesame seeds	$\frac{2}{3}$ cup sesame seeds
1-cm/$\frac{1}{2}$-inch piece cinnamon stick	$\frac{1}{2}$ inch piece cinnamon stick
2 cloves	2 cloves
4 black peppercorns	4 black peppercorns
pinch of dried thyme	pinch of dried thyme
3 large tomatoes (about 500 g/1 lb)	3 large tomatoes (about 1 lb)
1 onion, peeled	1 onion, peeled
1 clove garlic	1 clove garlic

Prick the duck all over, rub in salt and brown without fat (it has enough of its own) in a heavy flameproof casserole. Tip off excess fat and reserve it. Add the peppercorns, bay leaf, onion, garlic, and water just to cover and cook gently until tender (about 45 minutes). Remove the duck and set aside. Degrease the stock, keeping the duck fat in a little dish and the stock in a bowl for use later.

Soften the chillies in an ungreased heavy frying pan until supple and fragrant. Remove stalks and seeds and tear the chillies in rough pieces. Soak in hot water for about 20 minutes or until floppy.

Use the same pan to toast the sesame seeds, cinnamon, cloves, peppercorns and thyme, stirring occasionally, until the seeds are lightly golden. Set them aside to cool.

Grill [broil] the tomatoes, onion and garlic until blistered and soft. Quarter the tomatoes and onion. Peel the garlic.

Grind or blend cooled seeds and spices to a powder. Add drained chillies (or chilli powder), tomatoes, onion and garlic. Blend again until smooth. Add a little of the reserved duck stock only if necessary to release the blades.

Heat some of the reserved duck fat in a heavy flameproof casserole (which will accommodate both duck and sauce later) and fry the purée until thick and tasty, stirring and scraping well. Dilute to a light coating consistency with more stock, check the seasoning and put in the duck pieces. Simmer gently for a further 25–30 minutes or until the flavours are nicely blended.

Serve with *arroz blanco* (white rice – see page 143) or *tamales blancos* (steamed cornmeal parcels – see page 136), which make admirable sauce mopper-uppers, and some *tortitas de plátano* (banana fritters – see page 148).

Conejo a la criolla

RABBIT CREOLE-STYLE

Illustrated on page 129

The 'Creoles' are the descendants of the original settlers in Mexico, who – unlike the vast majority of Spanish colonists – did not intermarry much with the native Mexicans. The dish, therefore, shows more of the Spanish influence than the indigenous, though there are very definite Mexican touches about it. It's a rather good way to deal with rabbit, which – let's face it – can be rather dull and dry.

METRIC/IMPERIAL	AMERICAN
1 2-kg/4-lb rabbit, cut in 6–8 serving pieces	1 4-lb rabbit, cut into 6–8 serving pieces
1–2 tablespoons oil	1–2 tablespoons oil
75 g/3 oz hazelnuts	¾ cup hazelnuts
1 onion, peeled and chopped	1 onion, peeled and chopped
1 clove garlic, peeled and crushed	1 clove garlic, peeled and minced
3 large tomatoes (about 500 g/1 lb), peeled and roughly chopped	3 large tomatoes (about 1 lb), peeled and roughly chopped
2–3 fresh green chillies or drained canned *chiles jalapeños en escabeche*, seeded and cut in thin strips	2–3 fresh green chilies or drained canned *chiles jalapeños en escabeche*, seeded and cut into thin strips
250 ml/8 fl oz stock	1 cup stock
1 envelope (12 g/½ oz) powdered saffron	1 envelope (½ oz) powdered saffron
1 wineglass dry sherry or white wine	1 wineglass dry sherry or white wine
1 bouquet garni (parsley, thyme, bay leaf)	1 bouquet garni (parsley, thyme, bay leaf)
salt and pepper	salt and pepper
juice of 1 lime	juice of 1 lime
chopped parsley to garnish	chopped parsley for garnish

Dry the rabbit pieces well, then brown all over in the hot oil in a flameproof casserole and set aside.

Fry the hazelnuts (no need to peel the papery husk away) in the same oil. Lift out with a slotted spoon and leave to cool, then grind in a blender or food processor. Set aside.

Soften the onion and garlic in the same oil. Add the tomatoes, chillies, stock, the saffron dissolved in the wine or sherry, the bouquet garni, and salt and pepper to taste. Return the rabbit pieces to the casserole. Cover and simmer over low heat, or bake in a preheated cool oven, (150 c, 300 f, gas 2), for about 2½ hours or until the meat is flaking off the bone.

Stir in the ground hazelnuts and lime juice and simmer for a further 10 minutes. Sprinkle chopped parsley over the dish and serve with little boiled potatoes, and *acelgas con crema* (chard with cream – see page 156).

Page 129 *conejo a la criolla* (above), served with boiled potatoes
Previous page left to right: *tamales blancos* (page 136), *mole de guajolote o pollo* (page 124), *pato en pipián rojo de ajonjolí* (page 128), served with *tortitas de plátano* (page 148)
Left from the top: *torta de elote* (page 138), *habas en salsa verde* (page 157), *calabacitas con jitomate* (page 154)

VEGETABLES

Maize or corn, beans, squash and chillies have all been staples in Mexico for centuries and were introduced into Europe by the returning Spanish *conquistadores*. It was tit for tat, of course, for the Spaniards took with them to the New World such now firmly established foods as rice, wheat, broad or fava beans, carrots, cauliflowers, cabbage, spinach, chard and many others.

In Mexico, rice would usually be served before the main course (a 'dry soup') with other vegetables and beans being served after. However, I think it fits better into our scheme of things to serve any of these with the main dish to mop up sauces, and to provide colour and a bit of crunch. Don't be dismayed if some recipes look rather elaborate: almost all can be done in advance, and some (notably beans) positively benefit from being reheated.

STARCHY

Tamales	Steamed cornmeal parcels
blancos	plain
de calabacita con flor	with courgettes [zucchini] and their flowers
Uchepos	Fresh sweetcorn tamales
Torta de elote	Fresh sweetcorn torte
Frijoles	Beans
rollo a la veracruzana	rolled up bean purée (black)
de olla	pot beans (pinto)
refritos	bean purée (pinto)
frijoles veracruzanos	pot beans (black)
charros	pot beans with bacon and coriander
compuestos	smartened up tinned beans
Arroz	Rice
blanco	with stock, onion and garlic
con elote	with corn kernels
a la mexicana	with tomato, onion and garlic
verde	with green pepper, chillies and herbs
con caldo de frijól	with bean stock
Torta de papa	Souffléd potato cake
Papas con rajas	Sauté potatoes with chilli
Tortitas de papa	Potato pancakes
Tortitas de plátano	Banana fritters

El maíz

CORN

Maize or corn has been described as 'our greatest gift from the American Indians'* and forms the backbone of the Mexican diet in its various guises. There are hundreds of varieties, which fall into four main types: of these, the 'popcorn' and 'sweetcorn' types are self-explanatory. Then come the 'flint-flour' types, too hard to grind dry, but which can be softened by boiling in lime water and then milled, and by which means the average Mexican gets his daily 'bread' (i.e. his *tortillas* and *tamales*). The last type, the 'dent' type, is a very hard variety only suitable for animal fodder and is by far the most widely grown. In fact, if you've ever done a lightning raid on the local farmer's roadside corn cobs and borne them off home optimistically to eat dripping with butter, only to break a few teeth, now you know why . . .

In the recipes that follow, the *tamales* use cornmeal milled from the flint-flour types of maize, while sweetcorn crops up in the various delectable pies and semi-soufflés. It's worth noting that corn-on-the-cob would never be served within the context of a Mexican meal as we know it, although you might well meet it on a street corner, impaled on a sharp wooden stick, to be eaten like a lollipop.

TAMALES

STEAMED CORNMEAL PARCELS

The memory of good *tamales* can haunt you for years; unfortunately, the memory of bad ones (especially those which come in cans) can give you nightmares and indigestion. Properly made, they are one of the glories of Mexican cooking, and each area of Mexico has its own speciality. They are a sort of little steamed sponge-dumpling made with lard or vegetable shortening creamed to a fluff with *tortilla* flour and stock, and can be left plain (especially when served as a vegetable accompaniment as for *mole*), or they can be filled: shrimps, chicken, cheese, pork, chilli strips, vegetables, even the ubiquitous beans. In most parts of Mexico, they are wrapped in dried corn husks and then steamed; in Oaxaca, Veracruz and Chiapas, however, they are wrapped in strips of banana leaf and steamed, which gives them a special and delicious flavour all of their own.

Tamales are very good-natured: they freeze well and take kindly to being reheated – in a foil package or foil-covered baking dish in a preheated moderate oven (180 c, 350 f, gas 4) for 20–30 minutes or until well heated through. You can't really overcook them, so it won't matter if you leave them longer. Leftovers can be sliced and layered with any of the Mexican sauces, grated cheese and cream (rather like the *budín azteca* on page 78) for a calorie-counter's dream supper, with a nice sharp salad.

*MAIZE, Ciba-Geigy Agrochemicals, Technical Monograph 1979, Ciba-Geigy Ltd., Basle, Switzerland

Tamales blancos

PLAIN TAMALES

Illustrated on pages 130–131

Illustrated on pages 130–131

METRIC/IMPERIAL	AMERICAN
150 g/5 oz lard or vegetable shortening	10 tablespoons lard or shortening
250 g/8 oz *tortilla* flour	2 cups *tortilla* flour
50 g/2 oz plain white flour	$\frac{1}{2}$ cup all-purpose flour
350 ml/12 fl oz warm water	$1\frac{3}{4}$ cups warm water
200–250 ml/7–8 fl oz stock	1 cup stock
1 teaspoon baking powder	1 teaspoon baking powder
2 teaspoons salt	2 teaspoons salt
20 dried corn husks, soaked in warm water for 30 minutes and drained, or 20 sheets greaseproof paper 20 × 16 cm/8 × 6½ inches	20 dried corn husks, soaked in warm water for 30 minutes and drained, or 20 sheets parchment paper 8 × 6½ inches

Cream the lard or shortening until light and fluffy, as if making a sponge cake. While it is creaming, mix the flours to a dough with the warm water, as for tortillas, and add the stock. Gradually add this mixture to the creamed fat with the baking powder and salt. Continue beating for a few minutes more until really light and well-mixed: a ball of the dough will float when dropped into a cup of cold water. It should be about the consistency of cake batter.

Place about 2 good tablespoonsful of the dough on the bottom end of a soaked corn husk (where the corn cob was pulled off) or into the middle of a paper sheet. Fold the sides up and over, and the ends up. Lay face down so they don't unwind themselves while you finish filling all the rest. If you have some spare corn husks, tear a few lengthwise into strips and use the strips to tie round the *tamales*, to secure them.

Set up your steamer: if you have no double boiler or pressure cooker, improvise by using a frying basket or deep strainer placed inside a large pan. The basket or strainer should clear the bottom of the pan by at least 3 cm/1¼ inches. Place a coin in the bottom of the pan, pour in water to a depth of about 3 cm/1¼ inches and bring to the boil.

Put in the folded up *tamales* (vertically if there are enough to support one another all standing upright, in which case they cook more evenly; otherwise horizontally, in layers). Cover with spare husks, a folded towel, and a lid or foil and steam for about 45 minutes to 1 hour. Be sure you don't let the water boil dry: the dancing coin in the bottom will fall silent if this happens, in which case add more boiling water. The *tamales* are done when on opening a 'parcel', the dough comes away cleanly from the husk or paper.

If made in corn husks, you can serve the *tamales* as they are, having explained to your anxious guests that only the inside is eaten, not the husks. Otherwise, unwrap them from the paper and reheat in a foil-covered gratin dish for serving. *Makes 20.*

VARIATIONS

Before closing up your dough 'package', you could bury into it: a piece of cheese+chilli strips *or* meat in a sauce *or* a teaspoon of sauce (especially *mole*).

Tamales de calabacita con flor

TAMALES WITH COURGETTES [ZUCCHINI] AND THEIR FLOWERS

This recipe was Socorro's, my chief Mexican cookery adviser (and expert hairdresser too, but that was sort of secondary . . .). Once we even cooked up our own corn kernels and bore them off to the mill to be ground into cornmeal for the best *tamales* ever. She was very superstitious and used to claim that if there was anyone in the house who was a little 'out of sorts', the *tamales* wouldn't cook properly or evenly. In this case, it was necessary to tie some 'earrings' (*aretes*) – thin strips of corn husk – on to the handles of the steamer to ensure that everything came out right. Skip the flowers if you really can't get them, but do include them if at all possible, even if you can't quite muster the required 40: they fleck the *tamales* with lovely little orange splashes and give a super flavour.

METRIC/IMPERIAL	AMERICAN
1 small onion, peeled and finely chopped	1 small onion, peeled and finely chopped
1 teaspoon lard or oil	1 teaspoon lard or oil
250 g/8 oz courgettes, cut in little dice	½ lb zucchini, cut into little dice
40 courgette flowers, roughly chopped	40 zucchini flowers, roughly chopped
2 tablespoons chopped fresh *epazote* (optional)	2 tablespoons chopped fresh *epazote* (optional)
salt	salt
150 g/5 oz lard or vegetable shortening	10 tablespoons lard or shortening
250 g/8 oz *tortilla* flour	2 cups *tortilla* flour
50 g/2 oz plain white flour	½ cup all-purpose flour
450–500 ml/15–16 fl oz warm stock or water	2–2½ cups warm stock or water
1 teaspoon baking powder	1 teaspoon baking powder
20 dried corn husks, soaked in warm water for 30 minutes and drained, or 20 sheets greaseproof paper 20 × 16 cm/8 × 6½ inches	20 dried corn husks, soaked in warm water for 30 minutes and drained, or 20 sheets parchment paper 8 × 6½ inches

Soften the onion in the lard or oil without browning, then add the courgettes [zucchini] and flowers, *epazote*, if used, and a pinch of salt. Cover and cook gently until the juices render, then uncover, raise the heat and drive off all excess moisture. Cool a little.

Cream the lard or shortening until like whipped cream. While it is creaming, mix the flours to a dough with the stock or water. Gradually add this mixture to the creamed fat with the baking powder and 2 teaspoons salt. Add the courgette [zucchini] mixture. Continue beating until really light and fluffy: a small piece of the dough dropped into a cup of cold water should float, not sink like a stone.

Place a couple of tablespoons of the dough on the stalk end of each corn husk, or into the middle of the sheets of paper. Fold over the sides and turn up the ends to make a nice parcel. Steam following the detailed instructions in the recipe for *tamales blancos*, allowing 45 minutes to 1 hour, or until the dough comes away cleanly from the sides of the 'parcel' when you open up to have a peer.

Uchepos

FRESH CORN PARCELS

Uchepos come from the state of Michoacán, one of the most beautiful states in Mexico with a tradition for excellent food. They are like *tamales*, only instead of using cornmeal, they contain fresh corn kernels which are ground or puréed, then packed into the fresh husks from the corn, folded over into little parcels and steamed. They are my very favourite vegetable accompaniment, and provided you can get fresh corn with the husks still intact, they're no problem to make. They go very well with any of the dishes in tomato sauce, and are in fact often served as a separate course with tomato sauce, cream and strips of chilli.

METRIC/IMPERIAL	AMERICAN
3 corn cobs, preferably not too fresh, complete with green husks	3 ears of corn, preferably not too fresh, complete with green husks
2 teaspoons salt	2 teaspoons salt

Carefully unwrap the husks from the corn and set them aside. Discard the silk. Pare off the kernels with a sharp knife and grind with the salt in a food processor until about the consistency of porridge. (This can be done in a blender, but it may be necessary to add a little water or milk – not too much, it must be a stiff mixture.) Place a couple of tablespoons of the purée down at the base of each husk (where you pulled out the cob), fold the sides up over and double over the pointed end to enclose completely.

Line a steamer (see the recipe for *tamales blancos*, page 136) with spare husks, place the *uchepos* in serried ranks (if there are enough of them to support one another standing up) or lay them flat, making several layers. Cover with more husks, a towel and a lid and steam for 40–50 minutes or until the purée no longer sticks to the husk when you open them up to have a look.

Torta de elote

BAKED CORN TORTE

Illustrated on page 132

This simple and delicious recipe vies with the previous one for queen of the vegetable section: it is a sort of soufflé, golden brown and crusty on top, creamy and corny in the middle.

METRIC/IMPERIAL	AMERICAN
kernels from 3 corn cobs or about 500 g/1 lb frozen corn kernels	kernels from 3 ears of corn, or 1 lb (about 3 cups) frozen whole kernel corn
50 g/2 oz butter	$\frac{1}{4}$ cup butter
3 eggs	3 eggs
150 ml/$\frac{1}{4}$ pint milk or single cream	$\frac{3}{4}$ cup milk or thin cream
salt	salt

Preheat the oven to moderate (180 c, 350 f, gas 4).

Blend the corn kernels in a food processor or blender with the butter, eggs, milk or cream, and salt to taste. Tip into a lightly greased 1.5 litre/2½ pint [1½ quart] capacity charlotte mould or soufflé dish (or ring mould – it looks lovely when you unmould it).

Bake for about 1 hour, or until golden brown, firm and a skewer inserted in the middle comes out clean.

FRIJOLES

BEANS

'Beans, beans are good for the heart . . .'
A visit to the bean department of any Mexican market is a real feast for the bean-lover's eyes: mountain upon mountain of gleaming pulses, the shiny black beetle-like *frijoles negros*, the delicate yellowish-pink *canarios*, the pink and brown-flecked *ojo de cabra* (meaning, appropriately enough 'goats' eyes'), the huge multi-coloured *ayocotes*. All are loaded with protein, which probably accounts for the belief that the average Mexican peasant is considerably less undernourished than his counterpart in other parts of the developing world.

Nowadays, with the rediscovery of fibre as such a desirable element, plus the growth of vegetarianism, beans are enjoying quite a comeback. Try some of these recipes and you'll find a third reason for their popularity.

Rollo a la veracruzana

BLACK BEAN PURÉE IN A HEDGEHOG ROLL

METRIC/IMPERIAL	AMERICAN
1 quantity *frijoles veracruzanos* (see page 141)	1 quantity *frijoles veracruzanos* (see page 141)
2 fresh green chillies, seeded	2 fresh green chillies, seeded
1 onion, peeled and finely chopped	1 onion, peeled and finely chopped
1 tablespoon lard	1 tablespoon lard
50 g/2 oz crumbly white cheese	2 oz crumbly white cheese
3 stale tortillas, cut in little triangles	3 stale tortillas, cut into little triangles

Blend the cooked beans with some of their liquid in a food processor or blender until quite smooth. Set aside. Fry the chillies and onion in the hot lard until soft. Add the bean purée and cook, stirring and scraping, until very thick and quite dry – you should be able to roll it over and tip out on to a heated serving dish, like an omelette.

Scatter with the cheese and stick in the tortilla triangles at regular intervals, like a hedgehog's prickles.

Frijoles de olla

POT BEANS

The first maid we had, Audelia, stayed with us for nearly 4 years and we all wept copiously when she left to be a hairdresser. Her mother provided me with many a recipe sent via Audelia after a Sunday out, such as this one for pot beans. Don't soak your beans, whatever anyone tells you: it's not necessary and you lose some of the flavour, especially if you throw away the soaking water.

METRIC/IMPERIAL
250 g/8 oz dried pinto or red kidney beans
1–1.25 litres/1¾–2 pints cold water
1 small onion, peeled and quartered
2 cloves garlic, peeled and 1 crushed
2 tablespoons lard
1 onion, peeled and finely chopped
about 1 tablespoon salt

AMERICAN
1 cup dried pinto or red kidney beans
4–5 cups cold water
1 small onion, peeled and quartered
2 cloves garlic, peeled and 1 minced
2 tablespoons lard
1 onion, peeled and finely chopped
about 1 tablespoon salt

Put the beans in a large, heavy flameproof casserole with the water, quartered onion, whole garlic clove and 1 tablespoon lard and simmer for about 1½ hours or until nearly tender: if you lift out a tablespoonful of beans and blow on them, the skins will break open a little and wrinkle gently, and the beans will still have a bit of bite to them.

In a heavy frying pan on the next door burner, fry the chopped onion and crushed garlic in the remaining lard until nicely browned. Using a soup ladle, transfer one or two ladlesful of beans with their liquid into the frying pan, and fry hard, mashing with a wooden spoon, until really thick and well reduced. Tip back into the bean pot and add salt to taste (never add salt to beans at the beginning – you'll toughen them). Simmer a further 30 minutes until rich and tasty. They'll be even better next day.

Frijoles refritos

PURÉED AND FRIED BEANS

Illustrated on page 109

By preparing *frijoles de olla* (pot beans), blending them until smooth and then frying them until really thick and tasty, you arrive at *frijoles refritos*, which taste (and look) not unlike chestnut purée and make a marvellous vegetable accompaniment, as well as cropping up in many other recipes in the book (see *tostadas*, page 46, *chiles rellenos de frijól*, page 44, etc.). You can make them quite a bit dressier by moulding them, after frying, in a ring mould, covering with foil and keeping warm until needed. Turn out the purée and fill the hole with the chosen meat and sauce, or with *guacamole*.

METRIC/IMPERIAL	AMERICAN
1 quantity *frijoles de olla* (see page 140), or 2 400-g/14-oz cans pinto beans with their liquid	1 quantity *frijoles de olla* (see page 140) or 2 14-oz cans pinto beans with their liquid
1 tablespoon lard	1 tablespoon lard
1 onion, peeled and finely chopped	1 onion, peeled and finely chopped
1 clove garlic, peeled and finely chopped	1 clove garlic, peeled and finely chopped
grated Parmesan or Cheddar cheese	grated Parmesan or Cheddar cheese

Prepare the beans, preferably the day before. Blend them with some of their liquid in a food processor or blender until quite smooth. Use any remaining liquid to make *arroz con caldo de frijól* (see page 146).

Heat the lard in a very heavy, deep frying pan and fry the onion and garlic until softened. Tip in the blended beans and cook, stirring like crazy, till the whole mixture is really thick and pasty, so much so that you can roll it out on to a warm serving dish like an omelette. Scatter the grated cheese on top and serve with any of the meats with sauce, especially pork.

Frijoles veracruzanos

BLACK BEANS IN THE POT

Illustrated on page 149

All along the Gulf Coast and right round to the Yucatan peninsula, black beans are preferred to the pink ones of the highlands and the north.

METRIC/IMPERIAL	AMERICAN
250 g/8 oz dried black beans	1 cup dried black beans
1–1.25 litres/1¾–2 pints water	4–5 cups water
1 small onion, peeled and sliced	1 small onion, peeled and sliced
1 clove garlic, peeled	1 clove garlic, peeled
2 tablespoons lard	2 tablespoons lard
4–5 fresh *epazote* leaves (optional)	4–5 fresh *epazote* leaves (optional)
salt	salt
125 g/4 oz Parmesan cheese, grated, or crumbly white cheese	1 cup grated Parmesan or crumbly white cheese
very finely chopped onion	very finely chopped onion
chopped radishes	chopped radishes
chopped fresh coriander	chopped fresh coriander

Cover the beans with the water, add the sliced onion, garlic and 1 tablespoon lard and simmer for 1½ hours or until nearly tender. Do not add salt yet.

Using a large, wide frying pan, heat the remaining lard and fry about two ladlesful of the nearly cooked beans until quite thick and syrupy, mashing with a wooden spoon or potato masher. Tip them back into the simmering bean pot, add *epazote*, if used, and salt to taste, and cook for about another 30 minutes (although you practically can't overcook them).

To serve, sprinkle on the cheese, chopped onion, radishes and coriander: the white, red and green of the garnish looks nice against the shiny black beans.

Frijoles charros

POT BEANS WITH BACON BITS AND FRESH CORIANDER

METRIC/IMPERIAL	AMERICAN
250 g/8 oz bacon, cut in little pieces	½ lb slab bacon, cut in little pieces
2 medium tomatoes (about 250 g/8 oz), peeled and chopped, or 1 240-g/8-oz can peeled tomatoes	2 medium-size tomatoes (about ½ lb), peeled and chopped, or 1 8-oz can peeled tomatoes
handful of fresh coriander	handful of fresh coriander
1–2 fresh green chillies, seeded and finely chopped	1–2 fresh green chilies, seeded and finely chopped
salt	salt
1 quantity *frijoles de olla* (see page 140), or 2 400-g/14-oz cans pinto beans	1 quantity *frijoles de olla* (see page 140), or 2 16-oz cans pinto beans

Fry the bacon bits in a heavy flameproof casserole until the fat runs and they are crispy. Meanwhile, blend together the tomatoes, coriander, chillies and a little salt in a blender or food processor. Add this purée to the bacon, and fry hard, stirring frequently, for 10–15 minutes, or until well-reduced and thick.

Stir in the beans and simmer all together for a while longer to allow all the flavours to blend.

Frijoles compuestos

TARTED-UP CANNED BEANS

Canned beans are quite good in an emergency, especially if helped along a little in this way.

METRIC/IMPERIAL	AMERICAN
2 400-g/14-oz cans pinto or red kidney beans	2 16-oz cans pinto or red kidney beans
1 onion, peeled and chopped	1 onion, peeled and chopped
1 clove garlic, peeled and crushed	1 clove garlic, peeled and minced
1 tablespoon lard	1 tablespoon lard
1 large tomato (about 150 g/5 oz), peeled and chopped	1 large tomato (about 5 oz), peeled and chopped
chopped fresh *epazote* or coriander leaves (optional)	chopped fresh *epazote* or coriander leaves (optional)
chopped fresh green chillies *ál gusto* (optional)	chopped fresh green chilies *ál gusto* (optional)
salt and pepper	salt and pepper

Blend the beans with some of their liquid in a food processor or blender to a smooth purée. Set aside. Brown the onion and garlic in the hot lard, and add the tomato, herbs and chillies, if used, and salt and pepper to taste. Cook until quite thick and dry.

Add the bean purée and continue frying until well seasoned and thick. Turn out on to a heated serving dish and sprinkle on more *epazote* or coriander.

ARROZ

RICE

Rice, along with beans, is to Mexicans what potatoes are to us: in its various forms and colours it appears on almost every day of the year, and it's always delicious. In fact, before going to live in Mexico I always felt that rice was a bit dull, definitely not worth the calories. A few months there changed my mind. It's prepared in a slightly different way from any other I've come across: the rice is first soaked in hot water to loosen its starchy coating, then rinsed to remove the starch. It is then fried in what seems like an inordinate quantity of very hot oil, which is subsequently drained off. Then come the stock and flavourings, and the rice is left to cook fairly steadily until all the liquid is absorbed and the rice tender, but each grain fluffily separate. Try it – you may become a convert, like me.

Arroz blanco

WHITE RICE

Illustrated on pages 70–71

METRIC/IMPERIAL	AMERICAN
250 g/8 oz long-grain rice	1 cup long-grain rice
450–500 ml/15–16 fl oz stock or water	1¾–2 cups stock or water
1 small onion, peeled	1 small onion, peeled
salt and pepper	salt and pepper
5 tablespoons oil or lard	5 tablespoons oil or lard
1 clove garlic, peeled	1 clove garlic, peeled
1 fresh green chilli	1 fresh green chili

Soak the rice in a bowl of very hot water for about 15 minutes. Meanwhile blend together the stock or water, onion, and salt and pepper to taste in a blender or food processor until quite smooth. Drain the rice when the time is up and rinse under cold water until it runs clear. Shake dry.

In a heavy saucepan or flameproof casserole, heat the oil or lard to almost smoking. Throw in the rice and fry, stirring, for about 10 minutes or until glazed and sticky-looking. Tip off any excess fat (use a bulb baster or spoon, or tip the rice into a wire strainer held over a bowl, then put it straight back into the hot pan). Pour on almost all the stock mixture. Throw in also the garlic clove and chilli. Cover, reduce the heat to moderate and cook for 18 minutes.

After this time, there will be little holes all over the surface of the rice. The stock will be pretty well absorbed and the rice tender. Taste a bit: if it's still a bit hard, but all the stock is absorbed, add the reserved stock, cover and cook for another 5 minutes or so. Fork it up, check the seasoning, cover and leave alone for about 20 minutes to continue cooking in its own steam.

You can prepare the rice ahead of time, then either reheat it in its pan with a tiny bit more stock, taking care it does not scorch on the bottom; or you can tip it into a ring mould (for a *corona de arroz*), or place it in a serving dish. Reheat, covered with foil, in a preheated moderate oven (180 c, 350 f, gas 4) for about 20–25 minutes.

Arroz blanco con elote

WHITE RICE WITH CORN KERNELS

This can be prepared ahead of time and reheated in its pan. Or you can tip it into a ring mould (for a *corona de arroz*), or a serving dish, cover it with foil and bake in a preheated moderate oven (180 C, 350 F, gas 4) for 20–25 minutes.

METRIC/IMPERIAL	AMERICAN
250 g/8 oz long-grain rice	1 cup long-grain rice
450–500 ml/15–16 fl oz stock or water	1¼–2 cups stock or water
1 onion, peeled	1 onion, peeled
1 clove garlic, peeled	1 clove garlic, peeled
salt and pepper	salt and pepper
5 tablespoons oil, lard or dripping	5 tablespoons oil, lard or dripping
kernels from 1 corn cob, or 125 g/4 oz frozen corn kernels	kernels from 1 ear of corn, or ¼ lb (about ¾ cup) frozen whole kernel corn

Soak the rice in a bowl of very hot water for about 15 minutes. Drain and rinse well in cold water until the water no longer runs white. Shake dry. Blend together the stock or water with the onion, garlic, and salt and pepper to taste in a food processor or blender.

Heat the fat till almost smoking, then throw in the drained rice. Fry, stirring on and off, for about 10 minutes or until the rice is glistening and sticky-looking. Drain off excess fat. Pour on the stock mixture, cover and cook gently for about 15 minutes, by which time little holes should have appeared all over the surface, the rice will be nearly cooked and the liquid absorbed.

Fork in the corn kernels, cover and cook for a further 5–10 minutes or until the rice and corn are tender. Leave to rest, covered, for at least 20 minutes.

Arroz a la mexicana

RED RICE

Illustrated on pages 110–111

METRIC/IMPERIAL	AMERICAN
250 g/8 oz long-grain rice	1 cup long-grain rice
1 large tomato (about 150 g/5 oz)	1 large tomato (about 5 oz)
1 small onion, peeled	1 small onion, peeled
1 clove garlic	1 clove garlic
400–450 ml/14–15 fl oz stock or water	1½–1¾ cups stock or water
salt and pepper	salt and pepper
3–4 tablespoons oil, lard or dripping	3–4 tablespoons oil, lard or dripping
cooked or frozen peas (optional)	cooked or frozen peas (optional)
cooked, finely diced carrot (optional)	cooked, finely diced carrots (optional)

Soak the rice in very hot water for about 15 minutes while you prepare the rest. Grill [broil] the tomato, onion and garlic until blistered. Quarter the tomato and onion; peel the garlic. Blend together with the stock or water, and salt and pepper to taste in a food processor or blender till quite smooth.

Drain the rice and rinse under cold running water until it runs clear. Shake dry. Heat the fat in a heavy flameproof casserole or saucepan until almost smoking, throw in the rice and fry, stirring from time to time, until pale golden – about 15 minutes. Add the tomato mixture, cover and cook for about 20 minutes over moderate heat. By this time little holes should have appeared all over the surface, the rice will be nearly cooked and the liquid absorbed. Fork it up, taste for seasoning and stir in the optional vegetables. Cover and cook for a further 5 minutes, then leave to rest, covered, for at least 20 minutes. This can be reheated in the same way as the previous rice dishes.
Note: You could substitute a 250-g/8-oz can of tomatoes, drained and puréed, for the fresh tomatoes, but you may have to reduce the stock a little to allow for their wateriness.

Arroz verde

GREEN RICE

Illustrated on page 149

This is a particularly fetching rice dish, especially if moulded in a ring mould and the hole filled (after turning out) with *guacamole* (see page 34) or watercress – or the meat/fish which it is accompanying.

METRIC/IMPERIAL	AMERICAN
250 g/8 oz long-grain rice	1 cup long-grain rice
1 onion, peeled	1 onion, peeled
1 clove garlic	1 clove garlic
1 green pepper	1 sweet green pepper
1–2 fresh green chillies	1–2 fresh green chilies
handful of parsley or fresh coriander	handful of parsley or fresh coriander
350–400 ml/12–14 fl oz stock or water	$1\frac{1}{4}$–$1\frac{1}{2}$ cups stock or water
salt and pepper	salt and pepper
3–4 tablespoons oil, lard or dripping	3–4 tablespoons oil, lard or dripping

Soak the rice in a bowl of very hot water for 15 minutes. Meanwhile, grill [broil] the onion, garlic, pepper and chillies until blistered and soft. Quarter the onion; peel the garlic and pepper. Remove stalks and seeds from the pepper and chillies. Blend together with the parsley or coriander, stock or water, and salt and pepper to taste in a food processor or blender. You should have about 450 ml/$\frac{3}{4}$ pint [2 cups] of liquid altogether.

Tip the rice into a strainer, rinse well under cold running water until it runs clear, and shake dry. Heat the fat in a heavy flameproof casserole or saucepan to almost smoking, throw in the drained rice, and fry, stirring, till glistening and sticky-looking but not golden. Drain off excess fat, then pour in the blended mixture. Cover and cook over moderate heat for 18 minutes, by which time holes will have appeared all over the surface. Fork up and taste for seasoning, then leave to stand, covered, for about 20 minutes.

Pack the rice into a lightly greased (or nonstick) 1.25 litre/2 pint [5 cup] capacity ring mould. Press down well with the back of a wooden spoon, cover with foil and leave in a cool oven (110 c, 225 f, gas $\frac{1}{4}$) until ready to serve. Turn out on to a warm serving dish and fill with any of the above suggestions.

Arroz con caldo de frijól

RICE WITH BEAN STOCK

Never discard the bean cooking liquid from your pot beans (see page 140): use it for soup, or flavour your rice with it as in this recipe. If you use black bean broth for this dish, it goes especially well with any of the porks in tomato or chilli sauce; if you use pinto broth, it looks and tastes great with a creamy green chicken dish.

METRIC/IMPERIAL	AMERICAN
250 g/8 oz long-grain rice	1 cup long-grain rice
½ small onion, peeled and chopped	½ small onion, peeled and chopped
1 clove garlic, peeled and crushed	1 clove garlic, peeled and minced
4–5 tablespoons oil, lard or dripping	4–5 tablespoons oil, lard or dripping
500 ml/16 fl oz bean stock (from black or pinto beans)	2 cups bean stock (from black or pinto beans)
salt and pepper	salt and pepper

Soak the rice in a bowl of very hot water for about 15 minutes. Drain the rice and rinse well in cold water until the water runs clear. Shake dry.

Fry the onion and garlic in the hot fat until softened, then add the rice and fry for about 10 minutes. Moisten with the bean stock and season with salt and pepper to taste. Cover and cook for about 20 minutes or until the rice is tender and the stock absorbed.

Torta de papa

SOUFFLÉD POTATO CAKE

METRIC/IMPERIAL	AMERICAN
750 g/1½ lb floury potatoes	1½ lb floury potatoes
salt and pepper	salt and pepper
250 ml/8 fl oz milk or thin cream	1 cup milk or thin cream
50 g/2 oz butter	¼ cup butter
4 eggs, separated	4 eggs, separated
1 teaspoon baking powder	1 teaspoon baking powder
pinch of sugar	pinch of sugar
1 quantity *caldillo de jitomate* (see page 36)	1 quantity *caldillo de jitomate* (see page 36)

Preheat the oven to moderately hot (190 c, 375 f, gas 5).

Cook the potatoes in boiling salted water until tender. Drain, peel and mash with the milk or cream, butter, egg yolks, baking powder, sugar and salt and pepper to taste. Beat the egg whites with a pinch of salt until stiff but not dry. Fold into the potato mixture.

Spoon into a greased 1.5 litre/2½ pint [1½ quart] capacity charlotte mould or soufflé dish. (Can be done up to this point and set aside for up to 1 hour, with a large bowl inverted over the top of the whole thing.) Bake for 40–45 minutes or until golden brown, well risen and firm. Serve with the tomato sauce (unless the meat you are serving it with has its own sauce).

Papas con rajas

SPICY SPUDS: SAUTÉ POTATOES WITH GREEN CHILLIES

Illustrated on page 112

METRIC/IMPERIAL	AMERICAN
1 kg/2 lb small waxy potatoes (pink for preference)	2 lb small waxy potatoes (pink for preference)
2 tablespoons oil or lard	2 tablespoons oil or lard
1 onion, peeled and finely chopped	1 onion, peeled and finely chopped
2 fresh or canned green chillies, seeded and cut in strips	2 fresh or canned green chillies, seeded and cut into strips
salt	salt

Parboil the potatoes, then drain, skin and slice. Heat the oil or lard and fry the onion and chilli strips until soft. Raise the heat and add the potato slices and salt to taste. Fry briskly, tossing and turning, until evenly golden.

Tortitas de papa

POTATO PANCAKES

Even if you normally baulk at last-minute frying, these might be delicious enough to convince you that once in a while it's worth it. The potato mixture can be prepared ahead and left aside, covered, for up to 1 hour.

METRIC/IMPERIAL	AMERICAN
500 g/1 lb floury potatoes	1 lb floury potatoes
salt and pepper	salt and pepper
25 g/1 oz crumbly white cheese	1 oz crumbly white cheese
1 tablespoon finely chopped onion	1 tablespoon finely chopped onion
125 g/4 oz finely diced cooked ham or crumbled and fried chorizo (optional)	$\frac{1}{2}$ cup finely diced cooked ham or crumbled and fried chorizo (optional)
3 eggs	3 eggs
lard or oil for frying	lard or oil for frying

Cook the potatoes in boiling salted water until tender. Drain, then peel and blend roughly in a food processor with the cheese, onion, ham or chorizo, if used, eggs, and salt and pepper to taste.

Shortly before serving, heat oil or lard to a depth of about 5 mm/$\frac{1}{4}$ inch in a large frying pan. Drop the mixture by spoonsful into the hot fat and fry until golden brown and crusty on both sides. Drain on paper towels and serve at once, with a *caldillo de jitomate* (see page 36), unless to go with a ready-sauced dish.

Tortitas de plátano

SAVOURY BANANA FRITTERS

Illustrated on pages 130–131

METRIC/IMPERIAL	AMERICAN
3 large rather unripe bananas (about 500 g/1 lb), peeled	3 large rather unripe bananas (about 1 lb), peeled
1 clove garlic, peeled and crushed	1 clove garlic, peeled and minced
125 g/4 oz crumbly white cheese	¼ lb crumbly white cheese
salt and pepper	salt and pepper
2 eggs	2 eggs
5 tablespoons flour	5 tablespoons flour
1 teaspoon baking powder	1 teaspoon baking powder
lard or oil for frying	lard or oil for frying

Blend the bananas with the rest of the ingredients in a food processor or blender until smooth. Drop by the spoonful into shallow or deep hot lard or oil and fry until golden, turning once. Drain well on paper towels and serve with any of the pork or chicken dishes in sauce.

VERDURAS

GREEN VEGETABLES

As mentioned elsewhere in the book, vegetables would normally be served at a Mexican meal after the main course. However, we tend to prefer something with our fish or meat, and I have made suggestions accordingly for each of the main dishes. On the whole, the suggestions which follow are a little elaborate, but they can in almost all cases be done ahead of time which undoubtedly saves on last-minute saucepans and hassle. These vegetables go particularly well with the simpler roasted meats and grilled [broiled] fish or chicken, and some could even make delicious meatless supper dishes.

If, on the other hand, you prefer to serve a plain vegetable with your rather intricate Mexican sauce, be sure always to cook it in plenty of rapidly boiling, salted water and for the minimum of time. Drain and refresh under plenty of cold running water: this way you'll always have evergreen vegetables with a lovely crispness and bite. They can then be tossed in butter or steamed briefly to reheat just before serving time.

GREEN

Calabacitas	Courgettes
rancheras	with green peppers, chillies and corn
con jitomate	spicy ratatouille
rellenas de elote	stuffed with corn
torta de calabacitas	baked with eggs and cheese
Acelgas con crema	Chard with cream sauce
Chayotes rellenos de Veracruz	Chow chow or kohlrabi stuffed with eggs and cheese
Habas en salsa verde	Broad beans in green sauce
Budín de zanahoria	Carrot torte

CALABACITAS

Calabacitas rancheras

COURGETTES [ZUCCHINI] WITH CHILLIES AND PEPPERS

Illustrated on pages 70–71

There follows a slight profusion of courgette [zucchini] dishes, I know. Don't be dismayed – I think the suggestions cheer them up a bit, and since the squash family is native to Mexico, there's a wealth of recipes to choose from.

METRIC/IMPERIAL	AMERICAN
500 g/1 lb courgettes, sliced	1 lb zucchini, sliced
salt	salt
1 tablespoon oil	1 tablespoon oil
2 fresh or canned green chillies	2 fresh or canned green chilies
2 green peppers	2 sweet green peppers
1 onion, peeled and finely chopped	1 onion, peeled and finely chopped
2 cloves garlic, peeled and crushed	2 cloves garlic, peeled and minced
kernels from 1 corn cob, or 125 g/4 oz frozen corn kernels	kernels from 1 ear of corn, or $\frac{1}{4}$ lb (about $\frac{3}{4}$ cup) frozen whole kernel corn
3 tablespoons finely chopped fresh *epazote* (optional)	3 tablespoons finely chopped fresh *epazote* (optional)

Sprinkle the courgette [zucchini] slices with salt and leave to drain for 20 minutes. Pat the slices dry with paper towels, then fry on both sides in the hot oil in a frying pan. Remove.

Grill [broil] the fresh chillies and green peppers until blistered and soft. Peel the peppers. Remove stalks and seeds from the peppers and chillies and cut into thin lengthwise strips.

Soften the onion and garlic in the oil in the frying pan without browning. Add the chilli and pepper strips, corn and *epazote*, if used. Cover and cook for 10 minutes, then uncover and cook a further 5 minutes. Add the courgettes [zucchini] and salt to taste. Stir fry for a few minutes more, but don't overdo it, as otherwise the vegetables will lose their lovely bite and colour.

Page 149 from the top: *frijoles veracruzanos* (page 141); *arroz verde* (page 145), served in a ring mould with *guacamole* (page 34); *acelgas con crema* (page 156)
Previous page clockwise, from the left: *tarta de limón* (page 171), *flan de castañas* (page 165), *queso napolitano* (page 166), served with fresh strawberries
Left clockwise, from the left: *nieve de piña*, *nieve de limón*, *nieve de mango* (pages 160–1)

Calabacitas con jitomate

COURGETTES [ZUCCHINI] WITH TOMATO

Illustrated on page 132

This is a sort of Mexican *ratatouille* but with a bit of extra punch.

METRIC/IMPERIAL
500 g/1 lb courgettes, sliced
salt and pepper
2 tablespoons oil
1 onion, peeled and sliced
1 clove garlic, peeled and crushed
1 green pepper, grilled, peeled and cut in
  strips (see page 54)
2 fresh green chillies, cut in strips
3 large tomatoes (about 500 g/1 lb), peeled
  and chopped
chopped fresh coriander

AMERICAN
1 lb zucchini, sliced
salt and pepper
2 tablespoons oil
1 onion, peeled and sliced
1 clove garlic, peeled and minced
1 sweet green pepper, broiled, peeled and
  cut into strips (see page 54)
2 fresh green chilies, cut into strips
3 large tomatoes (about 1 lb), peeled and
  chopped
chopped fresh coriander

Sprinkle the courgette [zucchini] slices with salt and leave to drain for 20 minutes. Pat the slices dry with paper towels, then fry in the hot oil on both sides until lightly golden. Set aside.

In the same pan, soften the onion and garlic without browning. Add the pepper and chilli strips, and salt and pepper to taste, cover and cook gently until soft (about 10 minutes). Stir in the tomatoes and coriander. Cover again and continue cooking until the juices render (about 10 minutes), then raise the heat and cook briskly to evaporate the juices.

Stir in the courgettes [zucchini] and give the whole thing a final simmer together for about 5–10 minutes more.

Calabacitas rellenas de elote

CORN-STUFFED COURGETTES [ZUCCHINI]

METRIC/IMPERIAL
750 g/1½ lb courgettes (preferably round
  ones – see Glossary – but long ones will
  do)
salt
1 onion, peeled and chopped
1–2 fresh green chillies, cut in thin strips
1 tablespoon oil
kernels from 2 corn cobs, or 350 g/12 oz
  frozen corn kernels
2 eggs
3 tablespoons double cream or *crème
  fraiche*
50 g/2 oz Parmesan cheese, grated

AMERICAN
1½ lb zucchini (preferably round ones – see
  Glossary – but long ones will do)
salt
1 onion, peeled and chopped
1–2 fresh green chilies, cut into thin strips
1 tablespoon oil
kernels from 2 ears of corn, or ¾ lb (about
  2¼ cups) frozen whole kernel corn
2 eggs
3 tablespoons thick cream or *crème fraiche*
½ cup grated Parmesan cheese

Cook the courgettes [zucchini] briefly in boiling salted water. Drain and refresh with cold water to set the colour. Cut off the tops (or slice in half lengthwise), scoop out the centres and discard. Turn them upside-down on paper towels to drain.

Soften the onion and chillies in the oil without browning. Blend them together with the corn kernels, eggs, cream and salt to taste in a food processor or blender until the consistency of porridge. Add almost all of the grated cheese, but keep a little back to scatter on top.

Fill the prepared courgette [zucchini] shells and scatter on the rest of the cheese. (Can be prepared ahead up to this point.) Preheat the oven to moderate (180 c, 350 f, gas 4). Bake for 35–40 minutes or until golden brown and risen.

Torta de calabacitas

COURGETTE [ZUCCHINI] TORTE WITH CHEESE, MILK AND EGGS

Even my father, who has rather definite ideas about his food, thought this one was pretty good news.

METRIC/IMPERIAL	AMERICAN
500 g/1 lb courgettes, thickly sliced	1 lb zucchini, thickly sliced
salt and pepper	salt and pepper
125 g/4 oz crumbly fresh cheese, or	$\frac{1}{4}$ lb crumbly white cheese, or $\frac{1}{2}$ cup each
50 g/2 oz each Parmesan and Gruyère cheeses, grated	grated Parmesan and Gruyère cheeses
250 ml/8 fl oz milk	1 cup milk
2 eggs	2 eggs

Preheat the oven to moderate (180 c, 350 f, gas 4).

Cook the sliced courgettes [zucchini] in boiling salted water for 5 minutes until barely tender. Drain, refresh in cold water and dry on paper towels.

Blend together the cheese (reserving a little for the top), milk, eggs and salt and pepper to taste in a food processor or blender. Make layers of the courgettes [zucchini] and cheese mixture in a greased 1.5 litre/2½ pint [1½ quart] capacity charlotte mould or soufflé dish. Sprinkle the reserved cheese on top.

Bake for about 40 minutes or until golden brown, slightly risen and firm in the middle.

Acelgas con crema

CHARD WITH CREAM AND CHILLIES

Illustrated on page 149

This makes a very tasty accompaniment to a chicken dish or a roast, and can rather conveniently be done pretty much in advance. You'll find that with one chilli the dish is fairly mild; add the second and it'll be nicely warm. When testing this in a lesson once, we put in three and everyone was puffing and groaning . . .

METRIC/IMPERIAL
750 g/1½ lb chard, stalks and leaves
salt and pepper
1–3 fresh green chillies (see note above)
250 ml/8 fl oz double cream or *crème fraiche*
1 small onion, peeled and finely chopped
1½ tablespoons oil

AMERICAN
1½ lb chard, stalks and leaves
salt and pepper
1–3 fresh green chilies (see note above)
1 cup thick cream or *crème fraiche*
1 small onion, peeled and finely chopped
1½ tablespoons oil

Cook the chard in plenty of boiling salted water. Drain, refresh in cold water to conserve its lovely green colour, chop roughly and set aside.

Grill [broil] the chillies until blistered. Remove seeds and stalks, then purée with the cream in a food processor or blender until smooth. Add salt and pepper to taste. If the mixture is very hot, add more cream.

Soften the onion in the oil without browning. Add the chilli-cream mixture and cook, stirring, for about 5 minutes. (Can be prepared up to this point.) Just before serving, stir the chopped chard into the creamy sauce and cook just enough to heat through without overdoing the chard, nor losing its green colour.

Chayotes rellenos de Veracruz

STUFFED CHOW CHOW OR KOHLRABI

METRIC/IMPERIAL
6 *chayotes* (chow chow) or kohlrabi (about 1 kg/2 lb)
salt and pepper
1 small onion, peeled and chopped
2 cloves garlic, peeled and crushed
1 tablespoon oil or lard
1 large tomato (about 150 g/5 oz), peeled and chopped
2 eggs, lightly beaten
125 g/4 oz crumbly white cheese

AMERICAN
6 *chayotes* (chow chow) or kohlrabi (about 2 lb)
salt and pepper
1 small onion, peeled and chopped
2 cloves garlic, peeled and minced
1 tablespoon oil or lard
1 large tomato (about 5 oz), peeled and chopped
2 eggs, lightly beaten
¼ lb crumbly white cheese

Cook the *chayotes* or kohlrabi in boiling salted water until just tender (about 20 minutes). Drain, refresh in cold water, then slice off the tops and hollow out the flesh. Reserve the flesh and set the shells aside.

Preheat the oven to moderate (180 c, 350 f, gas 4).

Soften the onion and garlic in the oil or lard without browning. Add the tomato and hollowed-out *chayote* or kohlrabi flesh and cook, stirring, till rather dry. Tip into a blender or food processor and blend smooth with the eggs, most of the cheese, and salt and pepper to taste.

Fill the hollowed-out shells with some of the mixture (which, fairly logically, will be more than enough – use the rest for a quiche) and sprinkle the remaining cheese on top. (Can be prepared up to this point and set aside or refrigerated.) Bake for 30–35 minutes or until nicely risen and brown on top.

Habas en salsa verde

BROAD [FAVA] BEANS IN GREEN TOMATO SAUCE

Illustrated on page 132

I've tried to hold down on the green tomato sauce recipes, since the Mexican *tomate verde* is so disappointingly hard to find. However, this one I couldn't resist, and gooseberries make a pretty plausible substitute.

METRIC/IMPERIAL	AMERICAN
2 green peppers	2 sweet green peppers
2 fresh green chillies	2 fresh green chilies
1 kg/2 lb broad beans, peeled	2 lb fresh broad or fava beans, peeled
350 g/12 oz Mexican green tomatoes, husks removed, or gooseberries, topped and tailed	¾ lb Mexican green tomatoes (about 20), husks removed, or gooseberries, trimmed
1 small onion, peeled and roughly chopped	1 small onion, peeled and roughly chopped
stock (or cooking water from the beans)	stock (or cooking water from the beans)
1 tablespoon lard or oil	1 tablespoon lard or oil
salt and pepper	salt and pepper
120 ml/4 fl oz double cream or *crème fraiche*	½ cup thick cream or *crème fraiche*

Grill [broil] the peppers and chillies until blistered and soft. Peel the peppers. Remove seeds and stalks from the peppers and chillies.

Cook the beans briefly in boiling salted water until barely tender. Cook also the green tomatoes or gooseberries. Remove 3 tablespoons of beans to a blender or food processor and blend with the *tomates* or gooseberries, the peppers, chillies, onion and a little stock until smooth.

Heat the lard or oil to almost smoking and fry the sauce, stirring, until thick and tasty. Season to taste with salt and pepper. Stir in the reserved beans and the cream and simmer until nicely heated through.

Budín de zanahoria

BAKED CARROT TORTE

The baked vegetable 'pudding' (i.e. *budín*) is a great feature of Mexican cooking. This one will convert even the most hardened carrot-hater. I have also done it mixed with parsnips, though I don't think anyone in Mexico would have ever heard of such a thing.

METRIC/IMPERIAL	AMERICAN
500 g/1 lb carrots (or other vegetables), peeled and cooked	1 lb carrots (or other vegetables), peeled and cooked
50 g/2 oz butter	$\frac{1}{4}$ cup butter
pinch of sugar	pinch of sugar
2 teaspoons salt	2 teaspoons salt
3 eggs	3 eggs
50 g/2 oz Parmesan cheese, grated	$\frac{1}{2}$ cup grated Parmesan cheese

Preheat the oven to moderate (180 c, 350 f, gas 4).

Blend all the ingredients together in a food processor or blender. Pour into a greased 1.5 litre/2$\frac{1}{2}$ pint [1$\frac{1}{2}$ quart] charlotte mould or soufflé dish and bake for about 40 minutes or until firm, golden brown on top and a skewer stuck into the middle comes out clean.

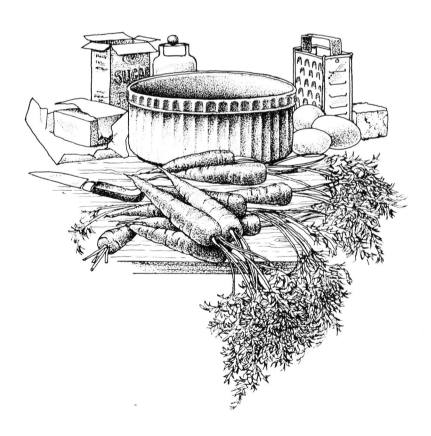

DESSERTS

After a Mexican meal, clearly what's needed is something very soothing. Many Mexican desserts, however, are a little too reminiscent of the nursery to be much fun, so I've held down on the jellied desserts and rice puddings so beloved of Mexicans of all ages. What more soothing could you ask for than, say, a sorbet made from one of the many tropical fruits available, or a *crème caramel* (*flan*), flavoured in one of a dozen ways? There are also some nice fruity and nutty possibilities, and an interesting sort of vegetable cake rescued from oblivion in the vegetable section of many a Mexican cookbook.

NIEVES

FRESH FRUIT SORBETS

Notes for all sorbets: if you can't get caster or superfine sugar which will dissolve just by blending it with the chosen fruit, it would be better to make it into a syrup first with the water, and then to add, cool, to the fruit base. Also, always take home-made sorbets out of the freezer and leave at room temperature for at least 1 hour before serving.

Nieve de piña

PINEAPPLE SORBET

Illustrated on page 152

If you really want to show off, you can carefully remove the flesh from the pineapple, leaving the shell intact, and use the shell for serving the sorbet.

METRIC/IMPERIAL	AMERICAN
1 medium pineapple (about 1 kg/2 lb)	1 medium-size pineapple (about 2 lb)
125 g/4 oz caster sugar	½ cup sugar
juice of 1 lemon or lime	juice of 1 lemon or lime
2 tablespoons Kirsch	2 tablespoons Kirsch
250 ml/8 fl oz water	1 cup water
1 egg white	1 egg white

Empty out the pineapple (see note above), or slice off the skin (don't worry too much about the little brown pocks – you'll be straining the puréed flesh later). Blend all the flesh with the sugar in a blender or food processor, then push through a sieve or food mill. You should have about 500 ml/16 fl oz [2 cups].

Tip into an aluminium charlotte mould (it freezes quicker) or glass bowl, add the juice, Kirsch and water and stir well. Freeze until semi-hard.

Beat the egg white till stiff and fold in. Whisk up the mixture really well until pale and snowy. Alternatively, tip into the food processor, add the unbeaten egg white and process until quite light and snowy. Freeze until firm.
Note: If not serving in the pineapple, decorate with twists of lime peel.

Nieve de limón

LIME SORBET

Illustrated on page 152

In Mexico, this sorbet would be tinted a delicate shade of green with food colouring – SUCH a pity. If you want to prove to anyone that it's made of limes, you'd do better to decorate with twists of peel.

METRIC/IMPERIAL	AMERICAN
350 g/12 oz caster sugar	1½ cups sugar
500 ml/16 fl oz water	2 cups water
grated rind of 4 limes	grated rind of 4 limes
juice of 6 limes (about 250 ml/8 fl oz juice)	juice of 6 limes (about 1 cup)
1 egg white	1 egg white

Make a syrup with the sugar and half of the water, simmering for 5 minutes. Add the lime rind and allow to cool.

Strain into an aluminium charlotte mould or glass dish, mix in the lime juice and remaining water and freeze until semi-hard.

Beat the egg white till stiff but not dry and fold into the sorbet, beating well until light and snowy. Or, tip into a food processor, add the unbeaten egg white and process until quite white and snowy. Refreeze until firm.

Nieve de mango

MANGO SORBET

Illustrated on page 152

Canned mangoes are about on a par with canned peaches. But fresh mangoes – now there's another story. The only possible reason for going to Mexico in May (in the thick of the rainy season) would be to sample a pale yellow *mango de manila* impaled on a wooden stick, the skin peeled down to resemble the petals of a flower, juice dripping down your chin, wrists, mango flesh up your nose . . . The best way to preserve this wonderful flavour, short of eating a mango lollipop-style as described above, is to make them into a sorbet or ice cream, where all the flavour is preserved.

Outside Mexico, mangoes are usually sold very green. Treat them like avocados, i.e. wrap in newspaper and leave to ripen in a warm, dry place.

METRIC/IMPERIAL	AMERICAN
2 mangoes (about 350 g/12 oz each)	2 mangoes (about $\frac{3}{4}$ lb each)
125 g/4 oz caster sugar	$\frac{1}{2}$ cup sugar
250 ml/8 fl oz water	1 cup water
grated rind of 1 lime	grated rind of 1 lime
juice of 2 limes	juice of 2 limes
1 egg white	1 egg white

Embed a fork firmly into the stalk end of the mango: you can feel if you've hit the stone, and should be able to push the tines of the fork well in to secure it. Then peel, keeping it still on the fork, and slice off all the flesh very close to the stone (which is like a hairy paddle). Don't try to remove the fork before cutting off the flesh, as the peeled mango is as slippery as a bar of soap.

Purée the mango flesh (and strain it if you think it's at all fibrous), then add the sugar, water and lime rind and juice and mix well. Freeze until semi-hard.

Beat the egg white stiffly, mix in and beat the ice really well until pale and snowy. Alternatively, tip into a food processor, add the unbeaten egg white and process until snowy. Refreeze until firm.

Nieve de papaya

PAPAYA SORBET

METRIC/IMPERIAL	AMERICAN
2 small papayas (about 350 g/12 oz each)	2 small papayas (about $\frac{3}{4}$ lb each)
125 g/4 oz caster sugar	$\frac{1}{2}$ cup sugar
250 ml/8 fl oz water	1 cup water
grated rind and juice of 2 limes	grated rind and juice of 2 limes
1 egg white	1 egg white

Peel the papayas and blend the flesh till smooth with the sugar, water, and lime rind and juice. Tip into an aluminium charlotte mould or glass bowl and freeze until semi-hard. Beat the egg white until stiff but not dry, fold into the sorbet and beat well until light and snowy. Or, tip into the food processor, add the unbeaten egg white and process until smooth. Refreeze until firm.

HELADOS

ICE CREAMS

Ice creams are usually made on an egg custard base, but I find this method of boiling a thick sugar syrup to the thread stage and pouring it hot onto the yolks is much simpler. There is no messing about with double boilers, as the yolks are thickened by the heat of the syrup, combined with the thorough beating they get. This base is then mixed with the desired fruit flavouring, plus cream, and away you go . . .

Helado de frutas

FRUIT ICE CREAM

This basic ice serves as a model. You can use any fruit you wish, sweetening the purée to taste before continuing with the egg yolk custard and the cream. Go easy on the sugar for the fruit, though, remembering that the sugar syrup will also sweeten it quite a bit.

METRIC/IMPERIAL	AMERICAN
125 g/4 oz sugar	$\frac{1}{2}$ cup sugar
120 ml/4 fl oz water	$\frac{1}{2}$ cup water
3 egg yolks	3 egg yolks
300 ml/$\frac{1}{2}$ pint double cream or *crème fraiche*	1$\frac{1}{4}$ cups thick cream or *crème fraiche*
500 ml/16 fl oz fruit purée, sweetened to taste (see note above)	2 cups fruit purée, sweetened to taste (see note above)

Dissolve the sugar in the water over gentle heat. Raise the heat and boil hard until the thread stage is reached – dip a fork into the sugar, wet your hand and take a bit of syrup from the end of the fork between finger and thumb. As you separate finger and thumb, a thread should form between them. The syrup will look quite thick and bubbly and the whole process should take 10–15 minutes.

Beat the egg yolks in a bowl until thick and light. Remove the syrup from the heat and allow the bubbles to subside before pouring on to the beaten yolks. Continue to beat until really light and mousse-like. Whip the cream until the beaters leave slight tracks. Combine the fruit purée with the egg yolk 'mousse' and cream.

Freeze, stirring once or twice during the freezing time to prevent the ice cream becoming granular.

FLAN

CARAMEL CREAM

Mexicans love *flan*. My father always claimed that this was because after the average Mexican marathon meal, it was about the only thing which would slip down without too much opposition. Whatever the reason, they are exceedingly popular and come in all flavours and shapes. Serve them with fruit compote or chocolate sauce and unmould on to a beautiful serving dish to lift them out of the nursery pudding class into something quite else.

Flan sencillo

SIMPLE FLAN

This recipe, Socorro's, gives a rather more solid result than the usual egg custard. The recipe and its detailed instructions serve as a model for the variations which follow.

METRIC/IMPERIAL	AMERICAN
50 g/2 oz sugar	¼ cup sugar
2–3 tablespoons water	2–3 tablespoons water
1 400-g/14-oz can condensed milk	1 16-oz can condensed milk
the same volume of ordinary milk (see recipe)	the same volume of ordinary milk (see recipe)
4 eggs, or 3 eggs and 1 egg yolk	4 eggs, or 3 eggs and 1 egg yolk
1 teaspoon vanilla essence	1 teaspoon vanilla

Preheat the oven to moderate (180 c, 350 f, gas 4).

Using a heavy metal 1.25 litre/2 pint [5 cup] charlotte mould, make a caramel in the bottom with the sugar and water, dissolving the sugar very slowly at first, then when the liquid is clear, boiling hard until a good golden. Set aside to cool. (You can do this in a heavy saucepan and then tip it into a soufflé dish, but you lose a lot of caramel and give yourself one more pan to wash.)

Tip the condensed milk into the food processor or blender, then fill the can with fresh milk and tip that in too, along with the eggs (or eggs and yolk) and vanilla. Blend until quite smooth.

Pour into the caramelized mould, cover with greased foil and bake in a bain-marie (water bath) for about 1 hour or until the custard no longer wobbles when you nudge it, and a skewer inserted in the centre comes out clean.

Allow to cool, then refrigerate until serving time. Unmould on to a serving plate.

Flan de naranja

ORANGE-FLAVOURED CARAMEL CREAM

METRIC/IMPERIAL	AMERICAN
175 g/6 oz sugar	$\frac{3}{4}$ cup sugar
2–3 tablespoons water	2–3 tablespoons water
4 eggs	4 eggs
2 egg yolks	2 egg yolks
1 tablespoon cornflour	1 tablespoon cornstarch
250 ml/8 fl oz orange juice (from about 4 oranges)	1 cup orange juice (from about 4 oranges)
thin orange slices, unpeeled, to decorate	thin orange slices, unpeeled, for decoration

Preheat the oven to moderate (180 c, 350 f, gas 4).

Using a heavy metal 1.25 litre/2 pint [5 cup] charlotte mould, make a caramel in the bottom using 50 g/2 oz [$\frac{1}{4}$ cup] of the sugar and the water (see the recipe for *flan sencillo* on page 163). Set aside to cool.

Blend or whisk together the eggs, egg yolks, cornflour [cornstarch], remaining sugar and juice. Let the bubbles subside a bit, then pour into the prepared mould. Cover with buttered foil and bake in a bain-marie (water bath) for 1–1$\frac{1}{2}$ hours or until set. Allow to cool, then chill before unmoulding and decorating with thin slices of orange.

Variation: To make your *flan de naranja* into a *flan de naranja con limón*, use the juice of 2 limes in place of one of the oranges to make up to the required 250 ml/8 fl oz [1 cup]. It gives the *flan* an extra piquancy which is quite delicious.

Flan de manzana

APPLE CARAMEL CREAM

METRIC/IMPERIAL	AMERICAN
50 g/2 oz + 2 tablespoons sugar	$\frac{1}{4}$ cup + 2 tablespoons sugar
2–3 tablespoons water	2–3 tablespoons water
500 g/1 lb tart apples, peeled, cored and sliced	1 lb tart apples, peeled, cored and sliced
1 teaspoon ground cinnamon	1 teaspoon ground cinnamon
25 g/1 oz butter	2 tablespoons butter
120 ml/4 fl oz rum	$\frac{1}{2}$ cup rum
juice of 1 lime or $\frac{1}{2}$ lemon	juice of 1 lime or $\frac{1}{2}$ lemon
3 eggs	3 eggs
250 ml/8 fl oz condensed milk	1 cup condensed milk
150 ml/$\frac{1}{4}$ pint ordinary milk	$\frac{3}{4}$ cup ordinary milk
1 teaspoon vanilla essence	1 teaspoon vanilla

Preheat the oven to moderate (180 c, 350 f, gas 4).

Make a caramel in the bottom of a 1.25 litre/2 pint [5 cup] capacity metal charlotte mould using 50 g/2 oz [$\frac{1}{4}$ cup] of the sugar and the water (see the recipe for *flan sencillo* on page 163). Set aside to cool.

Toss the sliced apples with the cinnamon and remaining sugar in the hot butter until golden and buttery. Moisten with the rum and lime or lemon juice and let them cool a little.

Blend or whisk together the eggs, condensed and plain milks and vanilla. Pour a layer into the prepared mould, then add a layer of apples. Continue in this way, ending with a layer of the egg mixture. Cover with a greased piece of foil and bake in a bain-marie (water bath) for $1\frac{1}{4}$–$1\frac{1}{2}$ hours or until the custard is set and no longer trembles when you nudge it.

Chill well, then turn out on to a nice round plate and serve with the best vanilla ice cream.

Flan de castañas

CHESTNUT CREAM

Illustrated on pages 150–151

'Surprisingly delicious' was the verdict of my students when we first did this one, after initial misgivings by all of us about 'heavy chestnut puddings'. The eggs lighten the whole affair considerably, and it looks marvellous on your best white serving dish with the chocolate sauce poured over and decorated with walnuts.

METRIC/IMPERIAL	AMERICAN
1 439-g/15-oz can unsweetened chestnut purée, or 2 220-g/8-oz packets frozen unsweetened chestnut purée	1 16-oz can unsweetened chestnut purée, or 2 8-oz packages frozen unsweetened chestnut purée
125 g/4 oz caster sugar	$\frac{1}{2}$ cup sugar
4 eggs	4 eggs
500 ml/16 fl oz milk	2 cups milk
1 teaspoon vanilla essence	1 teaspoon vanilla
walnut halves to decorate	walnut halves for decoration
sweetened whipped cream to serve	sweetened whipped cream for serving
SAUCE:	SAUCE:
150 g/5 oz plain or bitter chocolate	5 oz (5 squares) semi-sweet chocolate
125 g/4 oz caster sugar	$\frac{1}{2}$ cup sugar
250 ml/8 fl oz water	1 cup water
25 g/1 oz butter	2 tablespoons butter
pinch of ground cinnamon (optional)	pinch of ground cinnamon (optional)

Preheat the oven to moderate (180c, 350f, gas 4).

Blend together the chestnuts, sugar, eggs, milk and vanilla in a food processor or blender until smooth. Pour into a 1.5 litre/$2\frac{1}{2}$ pint [$1\frac{1}{2}$ quart] capacity charlotte mould or soufflé dish and cover with greased foil. Bake for $1\frac{1}{2}$–2 hours or until firm. Leave to cool in the turned-off oven, then chill well.

Make the sauce by melting the chocolate and sugar gently in the water. Raise the heat and simmer steadily for 10–15 minutes or until thick and syrupy. Stir in the butter and cinnamon, if used, and leave to cool. If the sauce thickens too much in the refrigerator, thin it down with a little water (or liqueur).

Unmould the *flan*, drizzle over some of the sauce, decorate with walnut halves, and serve with whipped cream. The rest of the sauce can be passed separately.

Flan de coco

COCONUT CARAMEL CREAM

Even dedicated coconut-haters will come round to this one, especially if you use freshly grated coconut, and serve it with an orange sauce. It is fairly solid: if you prefer a less firm *flan* increase the ordinary milk at the expense of the condensed.

METRIC/IMPERIAL
50 g/2 oz sugar
2–3 tablespoons water
1 small fresh coconut (to give about
  250 g/8 oz coconut flesh)
1 400-g/14-oz can condensed milk
120 ml/4 fl oz ordinary milk (or the coconut
  milk)
3 eggs

AMERICAN
¼ cup sugar
2–3 tablespoons water
1 small fresh coconut (to give about ½ lb
  coconut flesh)
1 16-oz can condensed milk
½ cup ordinary milk (or the coconut milk)
3 eggs

Preheat the oven to moderate (180 c, 350 f, gas 4).

Make a caramel in the bottom of a 1.25 litre/2 pint [5 cup] capacity metal charlotte mould with the sugar and water (see the recipe for *flan sencillo* on page 163). Set aside to cool.

Pierce the 'eyes' in the coconut and pour out the milk. Reserve it, if using. Crack the nut, extract the flesh and peel away the brown skin. Grate the flesh (a food processor works well).

Blend together the condensed milk, ordinary milk or coconut milk, eggs, and grated coconut in a food processor or blender. Pour into the prepared mould, cover with buttered foil and bake in a bain-marie (water bath) for about 1½ hours or until set.

Chill well, then unmould before serving.

Queso napolitano

YOLKLESS, ALMOND CARAMEL CREAM

Illustrated on pages 150–151

The next time you have a glut of egg whites and want a change from the inevitable meringue safety net, try this lovely light, nutty dessert. It looks particularly pretty if you unmould it and serve surrounded by a plum compote or fresh strawberries, their sharp red against the pale creamy white of the *queso*.

METRIC/IMPERIAL
175 g/6 oz sugar
2–3 tablespoons water
50 g/2 oz blanched almonds
500 ml/16 fl oz milk
2 tablespoons Kirsch
4 egg whites
pinch of cream of tartar or salt

AMERICAN
¾ cup sugar
2–3 tablespoons water
½ cup blanched almonds
2 cups milk
2 tablespoons Kirsch
4 egg whites
pinch of cream of tartar or salt

Preheat the oven to moderate (180 c, 350 f, gas 4).

Make a caramel in the bottom of a 1.25 litre/2 pint [5 cup] capacity metal charlotte mould with 50 g/2 oz [¼ cup] of the sugar and the water (see the recipe for *flan sencillo* on page 163). Set aside to cool.

Grind the almonds (not too finely) in a food processor, then put them in a nonstick pan with the milk and remaining sugar. Simmer gently for about 15 minutes, taking care the milk does not boil over. Leave to cool, then stir in the Kirsch.

Beat the egg whites until stiff but not dry with the cream of tartar or salt. Fold them into the almond-milk mixture, then tip the whole thing into the prepared mould. Cover with a buttered piece of foil and bake in a bain-marie (water bath) for 1¼–1½ hours, or until a skewer inserted in the centre comes out clean and the custard no longer trembles when you nudge it.

Chill well, then turn out and serve surrounded by a fruit compote or fresh strawberries or cherries.

Mousse de mango

MANGO MOUSSE

METRIC/IMPERIAL	AMERICAN
2 teaspoons gelatine powder (1 packet)	2 teaspoons (1 package) powdered gelatin
1 400-g/14-oz can mango slices in thin syrup, drained	1 16-oz can mango slices in thin syrup, drained
125 g/4 oz caster sugar	½ cup sugar
juice of 1 lemon or 2 limes	juice of 1 lemon or 2 limes
1 tablespoon rum	1 tablespoon rum
175 ml/6 fl oz thick cream or *crème fraiche*	¾ cup thick cream or *crème fraiche*
2 egg whites	2 egg whites
pinch of salt	pinch of salt
grated chocolate and lime peel twists to decorate	grated chocolate and lime peel twists for decoration

Soak the gelatine in some of the syrup from the mangoes, then dissolve gently. Purée the mango pieces with the rest of their syrup, the sugar, juice, rum and dissolved gelatine in a food processor or blender till quite smooth. You should have about 500 ml/16 fl oz [2 cups]. Whip the cream until the beater leaves traces, then gently fold into the purée. Lastly, beat the egg whites with the salt to a soft snow and fold carefully into the cold purée.

Chill until firm. Serve decorated with grated bitter chocolate and little twists of lime peel.

Postre de nuez

PECAN DESSERT

METRIC/IMPERIAL	AMERICAN
750 ml/1¼ pints milk	3 cups milk
150 g/5 oz sugar	⅔ cup sugar
2 tablespoons cornflour	2 tablespoons cornstarch
150 g/5 oz shelled pecans	1¼ cups shelled pecans
3 egg yolks	3 egg yolks
ground cinnamon (optional)	ground cinnamon (optional)
few shelled pecan halves to decorate	few shelled pecan halves for decoration

Simmer together 500 ml/16 fl oz [2 cups] of the milk and the sugar (without boiling over, preferably) for about 20 minutes until slightly reduced.

Blend together the remaining milk, the cornflour [cornstarch], pecans, yolks and cinnamon, if used, in a food processor or blender. Add to the pan and cook, stirring, until boiling.

Pour into little ramekins or coupes and chill well. Decorate with extra pecans.

Postre de piña

PINEAPPLE DESSERT

METRIC/IMPERIAL	AMERICAN
flesh from ½ medium pineapple (about 400 g/14 oz)	flesh from ½ medium-size pineapple (about 14 oz)
125 g/4 oz ground almonds	1 cup ground almonds
pinch of ground cinnamon	pinch of ground cinnamon
125 g/4 oz sugar	½ cup sugar
4 egg yolks	4 egg yolks
16 sponge fingers	16 ladyfingers
150 ml/¼ pint dry sherry	¾ cup dry sherry
sultanas and ground cinnamon to decorate	golden raisins and ground cinnamon for decoration

Blend the pineapple flesh in a food processor or blender with the almonds, cinnamon, sugar and egg yolks, until smooth. Pour into a heavy saucepan and bring to the boil, stirring. Cook until fairly thick (like an apple sauce). Cool.

Moisten the sponge fingers [ladyfingers] with the sherry and lay half of them in a serving dish. Add half the cooled pineapple mixture, then the rest of the sponge fingers [ladyfingers] and the rest of the pineapple. Chill well, and serve with the sultanas [raisins] and cinnamon sprinkled over.

Postre de Virrey con mango

MEXICAN MANGO TRIFLE

The number of egg yolks and the quantity of sugar in the original recipe for this dessert was so inordinate that I'm sure it must have been a printer's error, or if not a guaranteed recipe for *crise de foie*. After much experimenting and messing about, here is my version. Trifle has a way of popping up all around the world: maybe this sort of *zuppa inglese* made its way from Italy to Mexico via Maximilian (fresh from Miramare), along with other more recent desserts in the Mexican repertoire.

METRIC/IMPERIAL	AMERICAN
2 400-g/14-oz cans mangoes	2 16-oz cans mangoes
1 tablespoon finely grated lime rind	1 tablespoon finely grated lime rind
125 g/4 oz caster sugar	$\frac{1}{2}$ cup granulated sugar
6 egg yolks	6 egg yolks
1 teaspoon vanilla essence	1 teaspoon vanilla
3 tablespoons Marsala or sherry	3 tablespoons Marsala or sherry
4 egg whites	4 egg whites
pinch of salt	pinch of salt
250 ml/8 fl oz double cream, whipped until thick	1 cup heavy cream, whipped until thick
1 tablespoon icing sugar	1 tablespoon confectioners' sugar
2 tablespoons brandy	2 tablespoons brandy
250 g/8 oz sponge fingers or slices of sponge cake	$\frac{1}{2}$ lb ladyfingers or slices of plain cake
slivered almonds and grated chocolate to decorate	slivered almonds and grated chocolate for decoration.

Drain the mangoes, reserving 250 ml/8 fl oz [1 cup] of the syrup from the can. Mix the syrup with the lime rind and sugar, and boil to the thread stage (see recipe for basic ice cream on page 162).

Beat the egg yolks until thick and light. Remove the syrup from the heat, allow the bubbles to subside and then pour it in a steady stream on to the yolks, beating constantly. Keep beating till the mixture is very pale and mousse-like. Fold in the vanilla and Marsala or sherry and set aside.

Beat the egg whites with the salt until stiff but not dry, then fold them into the whipped cream with the icing [confectioners'] sugar and brandy.

Place a layer of sponge fingers [ladyfingers] or cake in a nice, glass dish. Make a layer of mango slices on top, add a layer of egg mousse and finally a layer of whipped cream with whites. Continue in this way until all is used up, making sure you finish with a layer of cream. Chill well.

Decorate with slivered almonds and/or grated chocolate before serving.

Torta de almendra

ALMOND SPONGE CAKE

METRIC/IMPERIAL	AMERICAN
125 g/4 oz blanched almonds	1 cup blanched almonds
4 eggs, separated	4 eggs, separated
250 g/8 oz caster sugar	1 cup sugar
pinch of salt	pinch of salt
3 tablespoons fresh white breadcrumbs	3 tablespoons fresh white bread crumbs
25 g/1 oz sultanas	3 tablespoons golden raisins
1 tablespoon rum or Kirsch	1 tablespoon rum or Kirsch

Preheat the oven to moderate (160 c, 325 f, gas 3). Line the bottom and sides of an 18 cm/7 inch springform cake pan with baking parchment paper as the cake sticks with a vengeance.

Grind or grate the almonds, not too finely: they should have a bit of texture. Set aside. Cream together the egg yolks and sugar until white and fluffy. Stir in the prepared almonds and breadcrumbs. Beat the egg whites with the salt until stiff but not dry, and fold into the almond mixture with the fruit and liqueur.

Pour into the prepared pan and smooth over the top. Bake for 1–1¼ hours or until firm, and a skewer inserted in the centre comes out clean.

Torta de elote

CORN CAKE

These 'vegetable cakes' are usually included in the vegetable section of Mexican cookery books, so for ages I quite overlooked them. The addition of the lime and sugar glaze at the end is an unorthodox one, and gives a nice sharp sweetness in contrast to the creamy, crunchy corn.

METRIC/IMPERIAL	AMERICAN
kernels from 2 corn cobs, or 350 g/12 oz frozen corn kernels	kernels from 2 ears of corn, or ¾ lb (about 2¼ cups) frozen whole kernel corn
125 g/4 oz butter	½ cup butter
75 g/3 oz sugar	6 tablespoons sugar
3 eggs, separated	3 eggs, separated
3 tablespoons plain flour	3 tablespoons flour
1 teaspoon baking powder	1 teaspoon baking powder
75 g/3 oz mixed dried fruits (e.g. apricots, sultanas, etc.), chopped if necessary	½ cup mixed dried fruits (e.g. apricots, golden raisins, etc.), chopped if necessary
pinch of salt	pinch of salt
2–3 tablespoons icing sugar dissolved in a little lime juice	2–3 tablespoons confectioners' sugar dissolved in a little lime juice

Preheat the oven to moderate (180 c, 350 f, gas 4). Grease and flour a 16 cm/6½ inch springform cake pan.

Blend the corn kernels in a food processor or blender until the mixture resembles fine porridge. Cream the butter and sugar until light and fluffy, then add the egg yolks. Sift the flour and baking powder on top and fold in carefully with a spatula. Add the puréed corn and dried fruits. Beat the egg whites with the salt until stiff but not dry. Fold them carefully into the mixture.

Turn the mixture into the prepared pan and bake for 1½ hours or until pale golden, risen and firm to the touch, and a skewer inserted in the middle comes out clean. The top often cracks, but this seems to be standard for baking powder cakes.

Cool on a wire rack, then ice with the icing [confectioners'] sugar mixed with lime juice.

Tarta de limón

LIME CHEESECAKE

Illustrated on pages 150–151

METRIC/IMPERIAL
150 g/5 oz digestive or petit beurre biscuits
75 g/3 oz butter or margarine, melted
1 400-g/14-oz can condensed milk
250 g/8 oz cream cheese or quark
2 eggs
juice of 2 limes or 1 lemon
finely grated rind of 1 lime
1 teaspoon vanilla essence
lime slices (unpeeled) to decorate

AMERICAN
5 oz graham crackers or other plain
  cookies (about 2 cups after grinding)
6 tablespoons butter or margarine, melted
1 16-oz can condensed milk
½ lb cream cheese or quark
2 eggs
juice of 2 limes or 1 lemon
finely grated rind of 1 lime
1 teaspoon vanilla
lime slices (unpeeled) for decoration

Preheat the oven to moderate (180 c, 350 f, gas 4).

Grind the biscuits [cookies] in the food processor, then add the butter or margarine to bind. Press into the base of a 25 cm/10 inch flan tin [or quiche pan] with your knuckles until evenly covered. Chill until set. Or, for a firmer crust, bake blind for 10 minutes.

Blend together the condensed milk, cheese or quark, eggs, lime juice, lime rind and vanilla until smooth. Spread onto the prepared crumb base and bake until set – about 35 minutes.

Allow to cool, then chill. Serve decorated with wheels of very thinly sliced lime.

Tarta de mango

MANGO TART

METRIC/IMPERIAL
150 g/5 oz digestive or petit beurre biscuits
75 g/3 oz butter or margarine, melted
2 400-g/14-oz cans mangoes, drained and sliced
3 eggs, separated
grated rind and juice of 2 limes
1 400-g/14-oz can condensed milk
125 g/4 oz sugar
1 teaspoon vanilla essence

AMERICAN
5 oz graham crackers or other plain cookies (about 2 cups after grinding)
6 tablespoons butter or margarine, melted
2 16-oz cans mangoes, drained and sliced
3 eggs, separated
grated rind and juice of 2 limes
1 16-oz can condensed milk
½ cup sugar
1 teaspoon vanilla

Preheat the oven to moderate (180 c, 350 f, gas 4).

Grind the biscuits [cookies] in the food processor, then add the butter or margarine to bind. Press out in a 25 cm/10 inch flan tin [or quiche pan] with the knuckles. Chill until set. Or, for a firmer crust, bake blind for 10 minutes.

Place the mangoes in overlapping circles on the crumb base. Blend together the egg yolks, lime rind and juice and milk and pour over the mangoes. Beat the egg whites with the sugar and vanilla to a stiff meringue. Pipe a lattice over the top of the tart.

Reduce the oven temperature to cool (150 c, 300 f, gas 2) and bake the tart for about 35 minutes or until the filling is set and the meringue slightly golden. Chill well before serving in very small slices: this is extremely sweet.

Pay de piña

PINEAPPLE TART

In Mexico, this dessert would be decorated with meringue made from the leftover egg whites, but perhaps that's rather overdoing it . . .

METRIC/IMPERIAL
1 medium pineapple (about 1 kg/2 lb), peeled
125 g/4 oz caster sugar
1 tablespoon cornflour
3 eggs
juice of 1 lime
PASTRY:
200 g/7 oz plain flour
150 g/5 oz butter or margarine
2 tablespoons sugar
4 tablespoons iced water

AMERICAN
1 medium pineapple (about 2 lb), peeled
½ cup sugar
1 tablespoon cornstarch
3 eggs
juice of 1 lime
PASTRY:
1¾ cups flour
10 tablespoons butter or margarine
2 tablespoons sugar
½ cup iced water

Make up the pastry in the usual way and chill.

Preheat the oven to moderately hot (190 c, 375 f, gas 5). Roll out the pastry dough very thinly and use to line a 25 cm/10 inch flan tin [or quiche pan]. Bake blind for 10–15 minutes or until just set.

Blend half the pineapple flesh in a food processor or blender until smooth. Cut the other half of the pineapple in slices and reserve for decorating the tart. Bring the purée to the boil and allow to simmer while you combine the sugar, cornflour [cornstarch], eggs and lime juice in the food processor or blender. Pour the hot pineapple purée on to the sugar mixture, blend once again and pour into the prepared pastry shell. Bake for 40–50 minutes or until set. Serve chilled, decorated with the reserved pineapple slices.

Ate de membrillo

QUINCE CHEESE

The various *ates* or cheeses made their way to Mexico from Spain, and the idea was adapted to use the native tropical fruits, although of course the quinces came to Mexico along with the idea. This makes an extremely good end to a Mexican meal, where all you want is a little nibble of something sweet, perhaps accompanied by a little piece of sharp Cheddar.

Mexican recipes direct that you leave quince cheese to dry out in the sun for several days, but since quinces come into season in Europe in the autumn when sunshine is in rather short supply, this is hardly practicable – and actually not necessary. You can pour it into a straight-sided container and leave it, uncovered, in the refrigerator. It sets quite hard and keeps for ages.

METRIC/IMPERIAL	AMERICAN
2 kg/4½ lb quinces, peeled	4½ lb quinces, peeled
about 1.5 kg/3 lb sugar (see recipe)	about 3 lb (6 cups) sugar (see recipe)

Roughly chop the quinces, reserving the cores. Cover the cores with 500 ml/16 fl oz [2 cups] of water and leave on one side. Barely cover the chopped quinces with water in a large preserving or cast iron pan [or kettle]. Simmer steadily until soft and the water nearly evaporated (about 30 minutes). Cool a little, then blend in a food processor or blender, in two batches, until really smooth.

Weigh the purée and put the same weight in sugar into the preserving pan with the soaking water drained from the cores. Dissolve the sugar gently until clear, then turn up the heat, add the quince purée and cook, stirring from time to time, for 15–20 minutes or until really thick and pasty, and the spoon leaves a channel when scraped across the bottom. The paste will turn from a pale honey colour to a good warm brown.

Allow to cool a little before packing into straight-sided jars or moulds (you want to be able to unmould it later and slice it). *Makes about 1.5 litres/2½ pints [1½ quarts].*

Bibliography

Carbia, Maria A. de, *Mexico en la Cocina de Marichu*, Mexico, Editorial Eposa 1969

Child, Julia, *Julia Child and More Company*, Knopf, New York, 1979

Crewe, Quentin, *International Pocket Food Book*, Mitchell Beazley, London, 1980

Flandrau, Charles Macomb, *Viva Mexico*, Appleton & Co., New York, 1908

Gandia de Fernandez, C., *Cocina Mexicana*, ed. Mexicanos Unidos, 1978

Kennedy, Diana, *The Cuisines of Mexico*, Harper & Row, New York, 1972
  The Tortilla Book, Harper & Row, New York, 1975
  Recipes from the Regional Cooks of Mexico, Harper & Row, New York, 1978

Lambert Ortiz, Elisabeth, *The Complete Book of Mexican Cooking*, Bantam Books, New York, 1967

Molinar, Rita, *Antojitos y Cocina Mexicana*, ed. Pax-Mexico, Mexico, 1975

Nieto Garcia, Blanca, *Cocina Regional Mexicana*, ed. Universo, Mexico, 1980

Ramos Espinosa, Virginia, *Recetas para la buena mesa*, ed. Diana, Mexico, 1969
  Un menú para cada día del mes, ed. Diana, Mexico, 1972
  Segundo libro de menús diarios para un mes, ed. Diana, Mexico, 1974

Samano Tajonar, Laura, *Los mejores antojitos mexicanos*, Gomez Gomez Hnos. Editores, Mexico

Simon, Kate, *Mexico, Places and Pleasures*, Thomas Y. Crowell, New York, 1979

Towle, Judith W., *Recetas Favoritas Mexicanas*, Judith W. Towle, Mexico, 1974

Velazquez de León, Josefina, *Mexican Cook Book devoted to American Homes*, ed. Velazquez de León, Mexico, 1979

Index